PARENTING
&ASPERGER'S

PARENTING
&ASPERGER'S

A Practical Handbook
to Help You and Your Child
Navigate Daily Life

Michael Uram, MA, LMFT, LPCC

ROCKRIDGE
PRESS

Interior and Cover Designer: Monica Cheng
Art Producer: Samantha Ulban
Editor: Carolyn Abate
Production Manager: Michael Kay
Production Editor: Melissa Edeburn

Author photo courtesy of Glenn Inskeep

ISBN: Print 978-1-64876-046-4 | eBook 978-1-64876-047-1
R1

I dedicate this book to my wife and children—

Angelique, Grayson, and Cameron.

I love the adventures that we have together

and how much you have taught me about life.

Contents

Introduction

As this book was being written, parenting seemed to take on a new heaviness as a result of the coronavirus pandemic. We've spent months at home with our children, wondering when it will end. I have seen so many families face sadness, loss, and isolation. But through the darkness and loss, many families have found hope and enjoyment in surprising ways. As parents in quarantine, we've been able to re-center our families, better understand our kids, and have fun with them in ways we never had time for before.

To me, this adaptability is a reminder that hope is key to our survival. When your attention is focused on growing, on finding ways to accept the life that is here currently and slowly making things better, each roadblock becomes a manageable hurdle.

In this book, I'm going to share with you not only hope that your relationship with your child can get better, but also the tools you'll need to improve it. You'll learn what Asperger's means for your child and for you. You'll learn that Asperger's isn't a disorder to be cured, but a way of viewing the world, a perspective with its own strengths and drawbacks. And you'll learn how to understand your child's way of seeing things and how to support your child without denying or devaluing who they are.

The names and identifying details of the individuals in this book have been disguised. Any resemblance to any person is purely coincidental. The examples I present of the techniques I use in my practice were successful for many of my clients, not just one individual.

This book's advice and techniques are not guaranteed to work for you, your child, or anyone else. They are not intended as a substitute for consultation with a qualified health professional. As you implement the suggestions in this book, I recommend you also consult a licensed mental health professional with extensive experience working with autism, Asperger's, ADHD, anxiety, and depression. A therapist will be aware of many contextual factors important in determining which techniques may work for you and your family.

PART ONE

UNDERSTANDING ASPERGER'S WITHIN THE AUTISM SPECTRUM

1

Asperger's Syndrome and Your Child

If you picked up this book hoping to deepen your understanding of the ways Asperger's affects your child, you've come to the right place. This first section explores the common traits and features of the diagnosis, and it describes how this diagnosis is currently defined. It covers some of the controversy regarding the terminology as it introduces ideas and treatments that can lessen the intensity of living with Asperger's for your family. It will help you develop a better understanding of how your child views the world and of how best to help your child grow and thrive outside their comfort zone.

A Basic Definition

Though described as a developmental "disorder" or syndrome, Asperger's is better thought of as a condition that makes understanding social rules and communicating clearly difficult for someone. A person with Asperger's has sensory experiences that differ from those of people without Asperger's and is usually uncomfortable physically and emotionally with change and transitions.

If you've found yourself frustrated and confused by the behavior of your child with Asperger's, don't be hard on yourself. Conceptualizing the experiences of someone with an Asperger's profile can be difficult. Psychiatrists, researchers, and other experts have argued among themselves about the condition. From 1987 to 1994, Asperger's was largely unrecognized and was given the diagnosis of autism. From 1994 to 2013, children displaying symptoms of Asperger's were given the diagnosis of Asperger's. Today, that diagnosis again falls under the umbrella of autism. Although listed as a diagnosis in the 10th edition of the International Classification of Disorders (ICD), the 11th edition will replace that diagnosis with the following one: "Autism spectrum disorder without disorder of intellectual development and with mild or no impairment of functional language."

Although the name of the diagnosis may have changed, the characteristics have not. The diagnosis of Asperger's is based on two types of symptoms:

Communication and social issues: Children with Asperger's struggle to understand the intent behind people's words, whether the person speaking is an adult or one of their peers. These children may show very little interest in playing with other children. Kindergartners who have Asperger's have real difficulty when other children are not as patient with them as their parents are. They get frustrated that other kids don't understand what they say, and they feel left out by them. Teens with Asperger's struggle to work in group settings at school, and they misunderstand others' behavior. Following the context in a group chat or social media thread may also be hard for a person with Asperger's.

Restricted, repetitive behavior patterns: Doing the same thing over and over is satisfying to a child with ASD. Kindergartners typically love to explore different learning stations in a classroom every few minutes or so, but those who have Asperger's become overwhelmed by having to switch stations. They don't like moving on to something else, even if they would be moving on to something they enjoy.

Three behaviors are typical in kids with Asperger's.

Resistance to rules and norms: Teens with Asperger's especially prefer to control their activity, and they feel that they need to do things their way. They resist "normal" activities when they don't perceive a reason for them. They may exhibit behaviors that don't appear to have a purpose but can be very soothing to them, such as humming or chewing on their shirt.

All-or-nothing communication: A child with Asperger's may struggle when having to tell you about their day, and not in the manner of a sullen teen who rolls their eyes at you as you try to engage them in a conversation. Someone with Asperger's has trouble summarizing data. They will give you every detail they can think of, not realizing that you just want the most important points. Prioritizing what the listener would like to hear is so challenging for someone with Asperger's that they may prefer to say nothing at all. And yet, they tend to want other people to get to the point as fast as possible. Individuals with Asperger's are often annoyed by small talk and don't understand why people engage in it. (I'll sometimes explain to someone with Asperger's that people will make conversation to determine whether continuing to interact with the other person is safe.)

Low threshold for being overwhelmed: People with Asperger's have trouble filtering out sensory information most of us can easily ignore. As a result, ordinary activities and events are incredibly stressful to them. The unpredictability or unfamiliarity of a location or activity can also leave them feeling stressed.

As we move forward in our journey together, you'll see that making the effort to take your child's point of view will help you understand their behavior and help them succeed.

EVOLVING TERMINOLOGY

The first research on Asperger's was published in 1944 by Austrian pediatrician Hans Asperger. Living in Nazi Germany at the time of his research, Hans Asperger was possibly complicit in atrocities experienced by individuals with various physical and mental health issues. Evidence refuting and supporting this notion has been put forth; I encourage readers to examine the record to learn more.

In the modern era, the term *autism* was first defined in 1987 in the *Diagnostic and Statistical Manual* (*DSM*), the reference book psychiatrists and other mental health professionals use to categorize behavior and guide treatment. The manual described those with autism as having impaired imagination and difficulties with social interaction, communication, and behavior. In 1994, Asperger's Syndrome was deemed its own diagnosis and was added to the next version of the *DSM*. In 2013, it was grouped with symptoms referred to as autism spectrum disorder (ASD). This decision remains controversial to this day.

The term *Asperger's* is still in use among those who believe the symptoms fit into a category narrower than ASD. Some advocacy groups propose using *Asperger's profile* to support the idea that the condition is a biological difference, rather than a mental health disorder.

For the purposes of this book, I will refer to Asperger's and autism spectrum disorder (ASD, or "on the spectrum") interchangeably. I will also use the term *neurodiverse* to represent children who are diagnosed and *neurotypical* to represent those who don't meet the criteria for Asperger's. You'll also see the term *aspie*, an informal self-description used by some in the Asperger's community.

Hallmark Traits

Since 2013, Asperger's has been recategorized by the medical community as a form of autism spectrum disorder (ASD) with "severity level 1" or as "high-functioning autism"—that is, with no accompanying intellectual or language impairment.

Asperger's doesn't come with intellectual deficits. But sometimes it will impact the mental functioning and the sensory and emotional regulation of your child. Children with Asperger's experience social isolation, communication difficulties, and reasoning deficits. They also have to cope with a wide range of sensory experiences. Some kids find walking on their toes most comfortable, whereas others are very sensitive to sounds and textures. Most children with Asperger's experience dysregulated behavior—their senses become overwhelmed or underwhelmed in everyday settings. Unlike neurotypical children, they will often struggle with reasoning skills, such as appropriately using inductive reasoning when navigating moods and experiences. Nevertheless, to meet the criteria for a diagnosis, a person must have great difficulty in social situations and must exhibit behavioral patterns that lead them to have a relatively less fulfilling life and possibly to need some help from others to be successful.

GENDER AND SEXUAL IDENTITY OR EXPRESSION

In my practice, I strongly support all my clients in loving themselves as they are. I often tell them that my goal is to help them "be more you," rather than attempt to inauthentically fit societal norms, which is called "masking." Don't pretend to be something you aren't to fit in, get along, or avoid your parents' judgment. Many LGBTQ+ kids on the spectrum are bullied or made to feel worthless because of their gender or sexual identity. Some consider self-harm as a result of the intense pressure and religious guilt directed toward them. As a parent, you may have a hard time hearing that your child identifies as the other gender or nonbinary. Please know that your support is incredibly important to your child's development of self-esteem and self-worth.

Many parents I work with question the sexual orientation of their Asperger's child. They may notice that their child is not interested in dating, discusses being asexual, or is incredibly uncomfortable being thought of in a sexual way. Other children can be very sexually interested, bisexual, or pansexual (interested in a relationship with a particular person, regardless of that person's gender).

Listen to what your child tells you about their sexual identity and preferences. They need to discuss these thoughts with a person they trust. Hear them out when they reason through the messages their body is expressing. They were born this way. If you are uncomfortable, speak to another trusted adult or a therapist about your concerns. There is no right answer, just compassion and understanding.

In my experience, the aspects of Asperger's that children struggle with most are communicating their needs, enjoying group activities, understanding social norms, using nonverbal communication effectively, adapting to changes in routine, accepting any activity outside their usual routine, and overcoming intense emotional reactivity and polarized beliefs.

Let's take a closer look at these challenges and how they play out in a child's day-to-day life.

DIFFICULTY WITH SOCIAL INTERACTIONS

Many aspie children actually have a strong desire to connect with others, but doing so is incredibly challenging. Typically, the biggest obstacles are finding a way to tolerate small talk and learning to have a conversation outside their preferred areas of interest.

For a child with Asperger's, even a casual conversation with a friend becomes a minefield of hand motions, eye movements, and body movements that can be quite overwhelming and confusing. The child with Asperger's just wants to get to the point, while the neurotypical child wants to express their affective empathy—that is, to use physical expressions of comfort, such as hugs, smiles, a softened tone of voice, or even a friendly punch on the shoulder. Kids on the spectrum rarely use these behaviors and have trouble interpreting them.

If the exchange leads to the neurodiverse child being rejected, they'll feel that rejection very deeply. When a neurotypical child is rejected, they will first feel sad and then will usually attempt to change their approach and interact differently with another child. But a child with Asperger's won't make that change. Instead they'll do the exact same thing each time and become increasingly frustrated. If this behavior is left unaddressed, the neurodiverse child can become more and more isolated and angry at a world that doesn't operate the way they expect.

For children with Asperger's, the social world is a continuously unpredictable, unknown, and potentially dangerous experience. They not only struggle to interpret perplexing social signals, but are also confused when their peers often don't follow the rules that both neurodiverse and neurotypical kids are taught: Be kind to others, do not talk in class, listen to the directions, do not cut in line, don't use bad words. A child with Asperger's feels surrounded by a herd of rule-breakers.

SEEING EYE TO EYE

I often hear complaints from parents that their aspie child doesn't make eye contact with others. A neurotypical parent may feel that this behavior should be easy to change. It isn't. I have a lot of compassion for the child who looks at me and says looking at others in the eyes is tough because "my feelings are so strong. I look away so my feelings are not so strong." As a collaborative problem-solving therapist, I've come to realize that addressing this issue is more complicated than simply training a child to tolerate the distress of eye contact during a conversation. We'll talk more about this topic in chapter 4 (see page 71).

CHALLENGES WITH ATTENTION AND IMPULSE CONTROL

If your child has ASD, chances are very high they also have a diagnosis relating to attention or impulsiveness. Their difficulties with impulse control are displayed in what they say and do; for example, children with Asperger's often impulsively state things that social norms deem uncomfortable or inappropriate. They then become frustrated or embarrassed that they now must deal with the secondary issue that has arisen from their comment.

In school, issues arise because many children with Asperger's struggle to follow the pace of a typical classroom. They may try to rush through an activity, or assume unstated rules, or turn inward toward their own interests, ignoring the outside world. These behaviors can seem like difficulty in paying attention or grasping a general concept, which is why Asperger's and attention deficit hyperactivity disorder (ADHD) are both diagnosed. But more often, if a teacher asks the child with Asperger's to repeat back what they covered, the aspie child can repeat what the teacher just said almost verbatim, while the child with ADHD will jokingly say "What?"

Improving attention is challenging; improving self-regulation and emotional regulation is less difficult when parents lean into this principle: Avoid the language of consequences ("Get ready for school or no computer time tonight") and instead use skill-building and confidence-building language. The most popular method of doing so is collaborative problem-solving, a technique for compassionately compromising with your child through empathy and understanding. You address both your concerns and your child's. Your child reasons through a potential solution to resolve the concerns each of you have. This leads to a long-term solution to repetitive situations and challenging behaviors. Working this out on paper is also helpful; giving aspie kids a visual cue on how to regulate their emotions can be very successful.

HYPERSENSITIVITY

Have you ever been bothered by reflected sunlight shining right into your eyes or an annoying sound, like the buzz of a fly you can't catch? Or the stiff, itchy texture of a too-tight shirt collar irritating your neck? How about a faint, disgusting whiff of garbage coming from somewhere you can't identify?

Imagine these things happening every day and you have some idea of what a child with Asperger's goes through. Aspie children often have hypersensitivity to what they see, smell, and hear; things they touch; or how others touch them.

This sensitivity is referred to as a sensory integration issue, and it feels like someone has adjusted the sensitivity levels in the brain to the point the regular world becomes very overwhelming. When your senses are overstimulated, it can be incredibly difficult to focus on ordinary tasks like having a conversation, reading a book, or keeping calm. Sometimes other types of sensory input bring relief. Author and professor Temple Grandin, PhD, the most widely known autism advocate, has stated that sensory issues are key to the condition.

Sensory integration is now seen as a common symptom of ASD, thanks to pioneering work by occupational therapist and psychologist A. Jean Ayers, PhD. You'll find more information about sensory issues throughout this book.

STIMMING

Kids who rock back and forth, hand-flap, make noises, repeat phrases, or do other types of "stims"—repetitive stimulating behaviors—do so to soothe their body when feeling overwhelmed. Never shame these behaviors or show embarrassment over them. Stimming is a neurodiverse child's attempt to self-regulate, which they can come to understand as unusual but not wrong. Offering them other self-regulation techniques, rather than criticizing their behavior, can allow them to channel their energy in more socially acceptable ways.

EMOTIONAL SELF-REGULATION AND ANXIETY CHALLENGES

Children with Asperger's often have excessive anxiety about the world around them. A neurodiverse child can see the world as filled with unknowns that are likely dangerous and to be avoided. And even when those with Asperger's try to follow rules they don't understand, they're often frustrated to find that others don't follow these same rules.

No wonder so many kids with Asperger's have intense anxiety and depression. If the world seemed never to work the way we wanted, who among us wouldn't have the same symptoms? My goal as a therapist is to respect the different ways neurodiverse children experience the world and urge parents to do the same. This approach does not simply encourage these kids to comply with their parents' requests but also gives them the tools to regulate their emotions no matter the situation.

If your child seems to be struggling with anxiety issues, I strongly encourage you to seek help from a licensed therapist. Professional therapists can offer support and guidance to help your child work through anxiety when flare-ups occur. Marriage and family therapists, clinical social workers, psychologists, psychiatrists, and professional counselors are all trained in treating anxiety and depression but many do not know how to adapt treatment for individuals with Asperger's, so be sure to ask about their expertise with ASD patients.

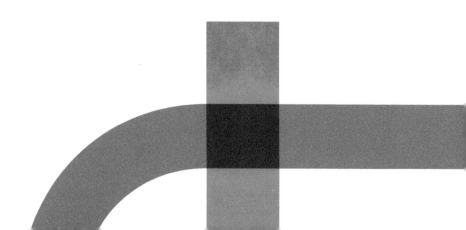

THE BIOLOGY BEHIND ASPERGER'S

Over the past few years, more and more studies have shown evidence for a biological basis of autism. Close relatives of individuals diagnosed with autism can show signs of autism while not having the condition themselves—that is, they display some social difficulties or inflexible behaviors. This suggests that certain genes are related to autism. In a 2019 study, researchers found that elevated blood levels of the neurotransmitter serotonin were a reliable sign for autism, also hinting at a biological cause. In other words, many parents of kids with Asperger's also have symptoms of autism or Asperger's.

One new theory on the biological basis has come from Henry John Markram, PhD, a neuroscientist at the École Polytechnique Fédérale de Lausanne in Switzerland. He conducted MRI scans of his family—including his son who was diagnosed with autism—and found that children with autism tend to have more intricate folds in certain areas of their brains. The significance of this characteristic is still uncertain.

The Path to Diagnosis

If your child doesn't have a diagnosis yet, that's okay. Examining the possibilities with books like this one is a good first step. What's important at this stage is that you're open to exploring whether your child's behavior is neurotypical. So many parents miss the signs of autism because they dismiss a potentially concerning behavior. The earlier you can identify these signs, the earlier you can start treatment.

FIRST SIGNS

Parents who suspect that their child may have Asperger's should see a doctor right away. Often the first step toward a diagnosis of Asperger's comes from the "Ages and Stages" developmental screening tool, a questionnaire typically given by your pediatrician with your child's annual physical exam through age five years. If the evaluation suggests your child struggles in some areas of development, even if they're not very behind, this directive warrants a follow-up. Discuss your concerns with your primary care provider to have your child evaluated as soon as possible. The earlier the child begins getting help, the better.

Though a child as young as 12 months may display symptoms, the most common time for a diagnosis is upon entering kindergarten, when struggles emerge related to attention issues or socialization, such as throwing tantrums or biting other children. If your child is experiencing these kinds of issues, I suggest meeting with their teacher and the school psychologist to explore possible explanations for, and options to help improve, your child's behavior.

The next-largest wave of diagnoses comes as puberty hits. Asperger's becomes more evident in this age group as social skills evolve and parents notice how far behind their child is socially, emotionally, and relationally. Often, a teenage child with Asperger's will either be avoidant of dating or (more rarely) excessively fixated on sexuality.

Regardless of when you acknowledge your child's behavior warrants an evaluation, the next step will be to contact a professional for an assessment. Your pediatrician can refer you to a specialist, therapist, or social worker who can administer most Asperger's or autism evaluations.

ADHD OR ASPERGER'S?

Self-regulation difficulties are common in children with ADHD and Asperger's. At the kindergarten stage, the two conditions can look very similar. One red flag is that children with Asperger's tend to have more emotionally intense meltdowns than those with ADHD. While children with both diagnoses will act out with tantrums and oppositionality, the duration of the meltdown is much longer for a child with Asperger's.

ASSESSMENTS

Very few assessments are available to diagnose Asperger's, and even fewer exist since the diagnosis became autism spectrum disorder. When I first started as a clinician, the most widely used assessment was the Gilliam Asperger's Disorder Scale (GADS) or Michelle Garnett and Tony Attwood's Australian Scale for Asperger's Syndrome. If a parent requests that I use either of these assessments, I do. While still reliable measures of Asperger's, both tools have significant flaws. Identifying Asperger's through an assessment measure is incredibly difficult.

The overall goal of an assessment for Asperger's is to determine whether your child truly has a serious condition. Before you seek out a specific assessment, however, ask yourself what you'll do with the diagnosis. If seeking school accommodations is one of your goals, be aware that the school will need to do their own assessment, including an IQ test. So you may want to start with a screening test—such as the Autism Spectrum Quotient (AQ) or the Childhood Autism (previously Asperger) Spectrum Test—and let the school perform a more detailed evaluation. In some cases, if your child meets the criteria for autism, you'll qualify for insurance to cover behavior therapy. Families who want a more certain diagnosis for that reason may opt for the Autism Diagnostic Observation Schedule, Second Edition (ADOS-2).

There are no established biomarkers for ASD—nothing that can be detected with a blood test, for example—so a diagnosis is made by a clinician who interacts with the child and observes them performing certain tasks. (Be aware that a few providers state that a biological marker is evident on a SPECT scan or a QEEG brain map. I have yet to see any large-scale blind test that backs up this claim.) A formal assessment will usually include a clinical interview with the professional who conducts the test. A psychologist may ask for a teacher evaluation, or even a classroom observation by a clinician, as part of their evaluation. Sometimes the process can feel overwhelming. But keep in mind that therapists and psychologists want to do their best to be certain their diagnosis is accurate. Thoroughness matters. I have yet to meet any professional who values insurance reimbursement or other factors over having as much certainty as possible about the child's condition. For the most part, the field is filled with compassionate clinicians.

Here's a list of the most prominent assessments for ASD, and other relevant tests, roughly in the order I'd recommend their use. Note that some public schools will reject any testing done outside their setting and will require you to take their tests (see page 17).

- **Autism Spectrum Quotient**, a good first step to establish if further assessment is needed.

- **Autism Diagnostic Observation Schedule, Second Edition (ADOS-2)**, to be certain of an ASD diagnosis. Lasting 40 to 60 minutes, this assessment is the most reliable for autism.

- **A physical evaluation** to rule out medical conditions that may mimic autism.

- **Wechsler Intelligence Scale for Children, Fifth Edition (WISC-V)**, to assess intelligence strengths and weaknesses that may be impacted.

- **A hearing test** to rule out auditory processing disorders.

- **An occupational therapist assessment** of sensory issues, which can guide treatment.

- **Children's Yale-Brown Obsessive Compulsive Scale (CY-BOCS)** to assess for symptoms of obsessive-compulsive disorder, which is common in autism.

- **Kaufman Assessment for ADHD**, which is also often seen in children with autism.

WHAT THE EXPERTS ARE LOOKING FOR

No matter what tests and assessments come into play, the goal is to identify symptoms that make life difficult for your child, yourself, and your family. The clinician conducting the evaluation can't use a test to determine which symptoms are most problematic, so an expert evaluator always explores the impact of any symptoms on a child's well-being, education, and family living. For example, if your child is often confused about whether their peers are joking or serious, their social life could be incredibly difficult because they can't following the pace and tone of a conversation. If your child's symptoms don't significantly affect any areas of their life, they won't be diagnosed with Asperger's.

That said, a few red flag behaviors do make an Asperger's diagnosis more likely. For one, many individuals with Asperger's are great at using sarcasm themselves, but have difficulty understanding when others are being sarcastic. Additionally, those with Asperger's often have a great interest in "programming life," meaning trying to find a way to understand, with absolute certainty, how to interact with fellow humans. They want to crack the code, as though life functioned like computer software. The neurotypical person intuitively understands that rules are flexible; an aspie wants rules that work without fail or exception. They become flustered when told that the rules of life are rarely consistent.

While these are red flags, I'd like to caution parents about one more behavior—having an intense interest in something—that many associate with autism, Asperger's included. I have met so many young people who've been shamed for their intense passion for a particular subject. If a child's intense interest is not causing any significant impairment in their life, I encourage parents to offer support, so long as their child has a healthy degree of other activities that they pursue. So many kids who love Pokémon, are good at remembering phone numbers, or are great at chess are mislabeled as probably autistic just because they have a passion for something.

What a Diagnosis Really Means

A diagnosis of Asperger's may not be the outcome you were hoping for, but having an answer means you're at the beginning of the story, not the end. Simple awareness of your child's diagnosis greatly improves your relationship with them. Your family will have to make changes, but even if the rate of change is one percent a day, eventually you'll see a significant improvement in your child's self-regulation.

What a diagnosis really means:

You have a starting point. Your diagnosis is an answer to the question of why your child has challenges. With that information, you can start to map the ways life can become less difficult for your child and for you.

Your child doesn't have to feel ashamed for being so rigid or for pushing away so many potential friends.

Your family can come together. Most of all, your diagnosis means that, as a team, your family can address the impact of Asperger's on all your lives, including finding your way into a new social group of other parents with similar questions, similar experiences, and similar fears.

What a diagnosis *doesn't* mean:

You're a bad parent. An Asperger's diagnosis isn't related to bad parenting. Similarly, putting off seeking a diagnosis for a while doesn't make you a bad parent either. The choice to bring your child to an evaluator can be tough.

Your child needs to be "fixed." This diagnosis does not lead to a cure but to an adjustment by the parents and an adaptation by the child.

Your child can't be held accountable for their behavior. I always emphasize to parents the importance of responsibility on the part of their aspie child. Empowering children to regulate their own behavior leads to long-term, durable change. Protecting them excessively often leads to fear of the outside world and anger toward the protecting parent.

PARENTS AND FAMILY RELATIONSHIPS

So, with a diagnosis established, what do you do now? My first answer is to pause, reflect, and observe how the world has changed. Thinking about your child with a label of Asperger's can feel overwhelming to many parents. But consider that the diagnosis really hasn't affected the current situation, other than putting a name to what you have already been observing. Over time, you will realize that not much is different. You are just more aware now. What the diagnosis does affect is your child's future, which will be much better now that you can understand the challenges they face.

Here are some actions to take in the early days of your child's ASD diagnosis:

Start a journal. One of the best things you can do as a parent is write down all the different thoughts you have on the first day you find out your child has Asperger's. During this journey, reflection will be a key component.

Remind yourself you're not alone. You're about to take on a different role in your child's life, which will take up more of your mental and emotional energy than you likely were planning for. But you're not the only one who has gone through this adjustment. There are thousands of other parents with experiences and questions similar to yours. In this book, we'll discuss options for connecting with other parents raising ASD kids.

Ask questions. Maybe you have doubts about the diagnosis. Maybe you don't understand what having Asperger's means. Maybe you're worried about how you'll handle things or the best way to tell friends and family. Whatever questions you have, big or small, I encourage you to ask the professional who is working with you. Ask every single question that comes to your mind.

Spread the word thoughtfully. At the start, it's best to let the people who love you and your child most know about the diagnosis. But the time may not be right to inform acquaintances or individuals you rarely interact with. Just like with any significant event in our lives, slowly getting used to the diagnosis allows for a less intense and more tolerable transition.

But remember that, ultimately, keeping the diagnosis a secret shames you and your child. Own the knowledge, leaving no doubt that you love your child. The most important opinion in this situation is your child's, so your main goal is to help them feel proud of themselves and to love themselves just the way they are. So when you feel you have the emotional capacity to manage their questions and reactions, let your extended family and friends know about your child's diagnosis. Include your supervisor or boss and work colleagues, so they'll understand when you have to take time off for doctor's appointments.

SCHOOL AND ACADEMICS

Aspie kids have great difficulty in a traditional school environment, but you can employ several strategies to improve their experience. Here are some important points to be aware of; we'll review more strategies for the school environment in chapter 5.

Push for an IEP. Having an Individualized Education Plan (IEP) is a necessity for a child with ASD. The process starts with requesting that your child be evaluated by the school psychologist. When you start this conversation, be prepared to be very assertive. You'll need a list of symptoms to share with the school. Your child's teacher may minimize the symptoms; if they can convince you that your child's difficulties aren't that bad, they won't have to do testing or give your child extra help. Be prepared, then, to emphasize the extent of your child's difficulties. (Try not to let this resistance antagonize you; ultimately, your child will benefit if you maintain a collaborative relationship with educational providers. Usually they do want to help but are constrained by budgeting and other limitations.)

Sadly, many schools I have worked with have gone to great lengths to delay this assessment, so don't be shy about pressing for faster action. Unfortunately, in some cases, the minimal support offered leads parents to pull their kids from public school and enroll them elsewhere or pay for the extra services on their own. For a more detailed examination of this problem and potential solutions, I recommend the book *Wrightslaw: All About IEPs* by Peter Wright, Pamela Wright, and Sandra Webb O'Connor.

Be prepared to trust. When things do go well, trusting the teachers and administrators at any school to follow through can be quite a leap of faith. But many educators will go above and beyond to help ASD kids fit in and feel safe in the classroom. I love hearing a great story of a teacher who listened to a child's needs and helped them learn effectively without needing prompting from others to do so. I also see how classroom size and curriculum expectations affect a teacher's ability to adapt their lesson plan for children with different learning styles.

Trusting teachers and education professionals to know what may help when your child has Asperger's is an exercise in patience and negotiation skills. Teachers are pushed to the limits of how many children they can manage in one classroom; they deserve patience and understanding. You also deserve to have your child's needs prioritized. This duality creates a potential conflict between assertively asking the teacher to spend more time adapting to your child's needs and not being unreasonable or offensive. Always keep your tone and language respectful, even when you're asking for more—or, rather, especially when you're asking for more.

Sweat the details. The adaptations an aspie child needs are much more nuanced than for a child with ADHD or other conditions. I've worked with schools on adapting the sensory environment, including regulating ambient noises by allowing the child to wear headphones or avoiding chalk that grinds on the board. Accommodations during unstructured time are also needed: assigning a lunch buddy to a kid who may be feeling lonely, or having a staff member organize a game with your child and other kids so they'll have a chance to socialize.

SOCIAL ACTIVITIES

Children with Asperger's often prefer individual activities. Paying attention to social cues, verbal cues, and nuanced social communication can feel so overwhelming that many of these children prefer the absence of communication over having to remember so many rules.

Neurotypical children will adapt to other children's social cues to be able to fit in and keep interacting until they find peers who are supportive and make good friends. Making this effort for children with Asperger's feels nearly impossible—or undesirable. Common among these children is a cognitive distortion called "overgeneralizing" that leads them to believe everyone is a bully if one child is. They often will resist changing to improve their social life. Here are some preliminary strategies to help a newly diagnosed child move toward being more social:

Try flipping the script. I have found that teaching children with Asperger's a trick I call "verbal judo" really helps them navigate a negative social situation. For example, if another child points out that the ASD child is walking on their toes, the ASD child can respond with, "Thanks for paying attention to the way I walk. How long can you walk on your toes for?" Most of the time the potential bully then walks away wondering how long they could walk on their toes.

Embrace the mundane. Most aspies believe that talking to others about their interests is the best way to connect with others; in fact, this approach is a much less successful path than just improving their conversational skills. I often encourage the aspie children I work with to try making interesting comments about any situation they're involved in and see if others respond better than when they talk about their latest interest. Sometimes I have them pretend they're an interviewer with comments such as: "You went to the new shop that opened? What did you like best there?" Often, the teenagers I help are surprised to discover their rather mundane comments or questions lead to acceptance.

2

Useful and Effective Treatments

Though Asperger's is a lifelong journey, there are plenty of ways to decrease the negative impact this condition has on your child. As we explore the many effective methods available, keep in mind that you get to decide which of them will work best for you and your child. Choose the ones that appeal most to you, try them out, and change the details as needed.

Effective Treatments

You may wonder whether there's real help for your child. There is. Each of the treatment options we're about to discuss is backed by science, and each has success stories from parents who've found them to be ideal for their child. I tell all my clients that there isn't one perfect solution; you'll likely land on a combination, with some interventions helpful at different developmental milestones, that can improve the quality of life for your child and yourself. This list isn't exhaustive, but it covers the most prominent options and will help you understand the range of possibilities.

Before we go into details about specific therapies, let's begin with a brief summary of each. Most non-medical therapies will require the direction of a master's-level licensed clinician, such as a LPCC, LMFT, LCSW, BCBA, PsyD, or PHD degree or certification.

- **Applied Behavior Analysis (ABA)** works well for 5- to 12-year-olds but is also great for ages 13 and up. This method is focused on applying behavior change techniques.

- **Collaborative Problem Solving (CPS)** helps kids see things differently and be more flexible, which works especially well for the 10- to 18-year-old child.

- **Early Start Denver Model (ESDM)** gives parents tools to enable their toddler to improve social communication while very young. The emphasis is on teaching communication and social skills to help the autistic child have a great time with others. This model is best suited to two-, three-, four-, five-, and six-year-olds.

- **TEACCH (Treatment and Education of Autistic and Related Communication Handicapped Children)** helps educators understand and celebrate your child's nuances rather than force them to fit into a mold. This model is best suited to two-, three-, four-, five-, and six-year-olds.

- **Cognitive Behavioral Therapy (CBT)** aims to show kids how their thoughts, behaviors, and feelings are interrelated, which helps with emotional regulation and reasoning skills. This technique works best for children 12 to 18 years old, but it can be adapted for children as young as 4 years old.

- **PCIT (Parent Child Interaction Therapy)** is really helpful for parents who want to know what to say and do in specific challenging situations with their child. The therapist literally guides the parent through the steps that will resolve a problem. This technique can even be done remotely. This technique is ideal for children 2 to 8 years old.

- **Medications** help children regulate their biology in a way that the rest of these interventions may not, so long as there aren't significant side effects. This choice is often difficult for parents to make. I always recommend gathering as much information as possible beforehand. Potential benefits, side effects, FDA recommendations, and the psychiatrist's experience with the medication are all incredibly important. I have seen kids thrive on medication that is carefully managed.

- Two additional treatment methods are worth mentioning because many have found them helpful, though I will not elaborate on them further: **Speech Therapy** and **Occupational Therapy (OT)**. Speech Therapy is often recommended for kids with Asperger's to improve prosody (tone of voice, rhythm, and flow of speech) as well as social and communication skills. Kids with Asperger's often have inconsistent rhythm, monotone voice, and pressured or fast-paced speech patterns. OT is useful for many kids with Asperger's who have difficulty with fine motor tasks, such as writing and tying their shoes and gross motor tasks, such as throwing and bicycling. OT also helps children improve their activities of daily living (ADL) skills such as brushing teeth, getting dressed, making the bed, and eating without making a mess. For more information on Speech Therapy, contact the American Speech-Language-Hearing Association (ASHA). For more information on Occupational Therapy, consult with the American Occupational Therapy Association (AOTA). Both of these therapies are incredibly important.

Applied Behavior Analysis

The first therapy most parents encounter when trying to help their aspie child is applied behavior analysis (ABA). The intent of ABA is to figure out what motivates the child to engage in a problematic behavior and to use positive or negative reinforcement; that is, apply consequences in response to a behavior in an attempt to effect change.

This explanation may sound complicated and clinical, but this therapy is not far removed from what many parents already do. A good example of ABA's positive reinforcement is teaching an eight-year-old to clean up their room. You might give them verbal praise as they pick up their belongings, and at the end of the cleanup, you allow them to play with their Legos as a reward. Whenever you study your child's behaviors and figure out how to shape them into what is healthy, you are using ABA effectively.

Many studies support the effectiveness of this therapy, showing that children do improve their behaviors by going through ABA. A challenge of the research is that studies measure whether the child performed a particular behavior, but don't establish how the child felt about doing the desired behavior. ABA can be done at home or in the school environment. For most children, this therapy is used in both settings.

Why This Therapy Works

ABA therapy, when used properly and in line with the theoretical model, really helps elementary school-age children figure out how to improve their social and self-regulation skills and enhances their ability to communicate clearly and effectively with others. The child gets a boost in confidence by receiving appreciation and the recognition that they pushed past their comfort zone and achieved a goal they did not think possible.

By acting as a scientist—that is, studying your child's behaviors to figure out what motivates them to be able to teach them how to adapt to their world—you're helping them make progress when they aren't aware enough to work out the best option for themselves. The therapy is very literal ("If I do A, I'll receive B"), with clear boundaries and expectations, and is quite appropriate for literal-minded chil-dren on the spectrum. For example, you might let your child choose their own outfit and dress themselves each day, without criticism or input from you, as long as they're ready to leave for school on time.

ABA isn't without controversies, mainly as a result of being applied inappropriately by poorly trained practitioners relying primarily on negative consequences to change a child's behavior. ABA should never be used to manipulate a child to do the desired behavior. Get your child's permission and input on what incentive they'd like to work for rather than unilaterally deciding that access to a preferred activity makes a good reward. Otherwise, they'll hide what they truly like for fear you'll use their preferences to control them.

This therapy works best for children who are younger and won't be aware of the techniques you're using—preschool to fourth grade seems to be the ideal age. For teenagers, this therapy can prove to be more challenging, as motivating an older aspie child by asserting control over their well-being is incredibly difficult. In fact, the adults with autism I've worked with have let me know this therapy really turned them off from wanting to connect with neurotypical people. They had come to believe others will manipulate them when wanting something.

Collaborative Problem Solving

Collaborative problem solving (CPS) is based on the theory that "kids do well if they can" and those who can't do well have lagging skills rather than a defiant, strong will. With this therapy, parents use compassion and attunement (aligning parents' emotions with their child's) to collaboratively solve the child's problems with them, creating long-term solutions to repeating problems. This theory came to prominence after Ross Greene's 1998 book, *The Explosive Child* challenged some of the approaches parents took with their hard-to-handle children.

The biggest hurdle with this therapy is trusting that your child's reasoning skills will improve if you give them the ability to control how to do things. For a parent, switching from having control over your child to trusting your child with control can be incredibly difficult (as every parent learns when their kid becomes old enough to drive a car). As a practitioner, I have seen many kids with ASD resist the process. They often don't trust that their parent will follow through. But with persistence, the process works. I have seen first-hand how this therapy can help parent and child be able to shift their perspectives and really connect with each other.

I like to start by having at least one parent and the child talk through a current concern around the house, such as the child refusing to clean their room. Each person takes their turn, showing empathy, understanding, and compassion toward the other, before anyone is allowed to talk about who's at fault. We then identify individual concerns and give each person as much time as they would like to explain their point of view. We finish by having each participant summarize the other's perspective, which is when we can focus on solutions.

CPS therapy shows that, whatever the situation, you have three plans for solving any problem with your child:

Plan A: Parent is in charge. "Do as I say. As a parent, I know best."

Plan B: Collaboration. "I'm going to show you empathy, ask what your concerns are, develop a few possible solutions with you, and we'll try one out for a week."

Plan C: Child is in charge. "I feel like we have too many issues we're trying to solve all at once; best not to correct this unhealthy behavior at this point. But know that in the future, as we make gains in other areas, we will come back to this behavior that needs to improve."

Each approach has benefits. CPS encourages us to stop relying exclusively on Plan A and consider other options. Often Plan B is the most effective method. Plan C is good to try after repeated failures.

Why This Therapy Works

This therapy can be incredibly effective if your child with Asperger's is inflexible, resists your guidance, and doesn't really care about rewards or consequences. CPS works because this therapy prioritizes educating a child on how to be a responsible adult, rather than reminding them of how irresponsible they have been. Avoidance leads to your child lying to you, which is bad. If you don't know about a problem they're having, you're not able to provide a fix. Another strength of CPS is that for each problem, you choose a plan that's going to work for both of you—for now. Letting go of any idea being a long-term or permanent solution makes compromise easier.

CPS can help when choosing clothes during a shopping trip, deciding on a college, or picking a restaurant. True joy can be found when you come to value your child's input as much as your own. The website ThinkKids.org, directed by the department of psychiatry at Massachusetts General Hospital, is a great resource for exploring CPS.

Early Start Denver Model

A diagnosis of Asperger's at an early age is rare, but some cases are identified early. For these kids, or those who show signs of Asperger's but don't meet criteria for a diagnosis, play-based interventions to help build social skills are fun and helpful.

The Early Start Denver Model (ESDM) helps young children, two to five years old, understand social and emotional concepts through play and peer interactions; this method has been shown to help kids improve their social, communication, and cognitive skills. The techniques are adapted from ABA therapy to encourage healthier social skills.

ESDM is designed to be used both at home and preschool, so children have a fun and positive experience practicing the same skills wherever they are. The child will be assessed at the beginning and regularly throughout to track their progress. As they progress, ESDM can be adapted to focus on especially challenging areas. The therapy can be used in a group setting or one-on-one. In practice, an ESDM session is very similar to the preschool curriculum a neurotypical child would experience. The therapy's biggest strength is that it feels like a typical day at school rather than a therapy session.

A strength of ESDM is a focus beyond just one area of a child's development, including language development, positive relationships, group activities, and tailored educational goals. One potential drawback, though, is that parent involvement is key. Some parents aren't able to follow through between sessions. Overall, the more the parent and therapist work together and families practice these techniques at home, the more likely the child's life will get better with this therapy.

Why This Therapy Works

Many practitioners have found that this therapy does help children rapidly improve their social and emotional skills, while also increasing their self-esteem. Parents are amazed to see their ASD child make strides in various areas while working with caring, compassionate professionals and educators. (I always suggest when considering a program, parents meet not just with the program director, but also with the individuals who will spend the most time with their child. These people will influence your child most.)

ESDM is effective because of the focus on comprehensively understanding a child and developing an education plan geared toward specific behaviors over a long period of time at an early stage of life. The high frequency with which a child is able to interact with their treatment team is also key; kids in the program are around their teachers or their behavior analyst most days. This immersion gives the children many opportunities to try out the different techniques they're learning and have a great time playing by themselves or with others.

Treatment and Education of Autistic and Related Communication Handicapped Children

More and more schools these days specialize in educating children with autism. The most widely used therapy on which schools draw is the Treatment and Education of Autistic and Related

Communication Handicapped Children (TEACCH) method, which helps educators understand and celebrate the nuances of each child. Developed at the University of North Carolina at Chapel Hill in the 1960s, the TEACCH education model is the gold standard for educating an individual with autism.

TEACCH emphasizes inclusion and self-determination. The core message to children is individuals with autism are different, and this difference is okay. Being a successful person does not mean someone with Asperger's needs to be just like a neurotypical person. You can be you, and be independent and happy.

TEACCH's basic principles for a successful structured education are:

- An individualized and family-centered plan
- Structured teaching that emphasizes a consistent physical structure, visual prompts and schedules, clearly defined work systems, and tasks organized in understandable sequences
- A wide range of strategies that work for the child with Asperger's
- Cooperation among the child, parent, and educator

TEACCH is known to be flexible, respectful, and successful. Each aspie child receives a tailored education whereby the child's strengths are used to address challenging areas. Educators make no assumptions about how the child learns. Rather, they adapt to each setback the child experiences, carefully noting exactly which step in the learning process caused a stall or struggle.

Why This Therapy Works

The TEACCH therapy method works because practitioners show a great deal of understanding of the strengths and weaknesses of neurodiverse students. The curriculum is then adapted to individually match each child's skill set, rather than expecting everyone in the classroom to learn in the same exact way.

TEACCH is likely the most widely used education model in the United States and United Kingdom for children diagnosed with ASD. Solid research shows this model works, though a few studies counter these claims. As this model continues to evolve, I hope researchers will examine ways to clarify the conflicting research and determine how to fine-tune this treatment.

This therapy doesn't force neurodiverse children to focus constantly on their deficits and insist they adapt to a neurotypical world. Instead, teachers are encouraged to have patience to adapt to challenges and really understand what the child's world is like to help them grow from there. To that end, the system breaks down new behaviors into steps and sequences. This practice really helps individuals on the spectrum, who respond well to clearly defined actions that lead to specific results.

Cognitive Behavioral Therapy

I've seen many parents use the above-mentioned therapies with only moderate success. The reason, most often, is that their child struggles with awareness of what they're doing and why they are doing it. A child with Asperger's may learn new, more acceptable behaviors but can remain unaware of how their behavior impacts others.

Cognitive Behavioral Therapy (CBT) is one way to change a person's self-awareness. Simply put, this therapy involves the process of understanding one's own thoughts (cognitive) and actions (behavioral) and the interplay of both to produce feelings. By changing thoughts and behaviors, mood can change. The simplicity of CBT makes this therapeutic model the one to which I most often turn in my practice. Instead of forcing someone with Asperger's to adapt to a neurotypical world, CBT helps them grow from understanding of their own world.

When individuals with Asperger's are overwhelmed by a situation, they can benefit from breaking down their thoughts with CBT techniques. Breaking concepts down into manageable pieces helps us reason through a situation with logic, rather than react

with emotion to what's happening. And logic-based thought pro-
cesses are much easier for an individual on the spectrum.

Additionally, children with Asperger's often are not aware of,
or ignore, their emotions when those feelings are small. Eventually their smaller emotional issues build into something big and
they respond with intense drama, acting out inappropriately. Then
they feel terrible about the way they behaved. CBT can teach a
child that their small feelings don't go away just because the child
ignores them; rather, feelings keep building until they become
overwhelming. But if we deal with our emotions in that moment,
they're more likely to melt away.

This concept works really well for teenagers who struggle with
relationships. CBT explains that cognitive empathy (telling someone you understand how they feel) and affective empathy (showing
someone how you feel) are equally important. Learning the connection between thoughts, behaviors, and feelings helps the aspie
understand that telling somebody you really feel for them without
physically comforting them or showing signs of sadness in your
tone of voice isn't nearly as heartfelt.

Why This Therapy Works

As I mentioned, most teenagers with Asperger's really respond
well to CBT. The science-based approach to feelings makes sense
to them and this therapy helps them realize they have been devaluing their emotions and overvaluing their thoughts. Learning
their emotions do have value is usually quite a surprise to them.
Elementary-age children really like CBT because this therapy gives
them words to describe how they feel. CBT breaks down some
pretty complex concepts that now make sense to children of this
younger age.

For example, suppose your child thinks they are a failure
because they did poorly on a school quiz. Their shame is 8 out
of 10. You encourage them to notice their core thought is "I'm a
failure." But the evidence shows this was the first quiz out of four
they've failed. More quizzes and a midterm are coming up and
these tests can help them turn their grade around. They can then

choose to study what they got wrong on the quiz and accept their mistakes. Their new, balanced thought is "I'm not a failure, but I sometimes fail." Their shame is now 3 out of 10.

Parents are drawn to CBT because it helps them explore some of their child's deep thoughts without judgment. I know many teachers who embrace CBT because it helps students change their view of school and of other people. CBT teaches the neurodiverse child to behave differently and gives them new insight.

Parent Child Interaction Therapy

Many a parent has jokingly asked if I could be available to them through a Bluetooth headset, telling them exactly what they should say to their child when a difficult moment arises. They tell me they often regret what they say to their child when they are frustrated and wish they had someone whispering the right words into their ear. Believe it or not, Parent Child Interaction Therapy (PCIT) is almost exactly this scenario!

The therapist meets with either the parent or the parent and child together, and directs the parent in the moment as the parent tries different strategies. The parent and child play in a room with a one-way mirror. The parent wears an earpiece, and the therapist uses a microphone to coach the parent as they interact with their child. PCIT is designed for kids between the ages of two and seven; the main goal is to increase the connection parents have with their child. This therapy helps parents who feel overwhelmed trying to manage their child's undesirable behaviors.

PCIT focuses on extreme behavior that happens when the child is dysregulated, or emotionally out of control: tantrums, meltdowns, and hitting siblings and parents. Rather than just telling the parent the theory behind the child's conduct, PCIT teaches parents how to respond, providing actionable, real-world guidance. This therapy is delivered in an office setting rather than at school or at home, though there's been a movement to offer telemedicine options.

Parenting a child on the spectrum can be incredibly frustrating when you don't understand what your child needs. All you can do is comfort them, show them warmth and compassion, let them see they can trust you, and praise what they do right. Learning these skills is the first phase of PCIT treatment. The second phase is a bit more complicated: The therapist walks you through a step-by-step approach to discipline aimed at keeping you confident, calm, and consistent. If you are dysregulated, your child is going to be as well.

Many children with autism have disruptive behaviors that can be very concerning and even dangerous. As a neurotypical parent, responding to these behaviors with consequences or frustration usually escalates the situation. PCIT slows this reaction and helps parents develop radical acceptance (see page 53) and guide the child toward a more positive and realistic outcome.

Why This Therapy Works

This therapy prioritizes interrupting the parent-child dynamics that often escalate into yelling and screaming by both parties. The central tenet is to give a structure to many interactions between parent and child where none had existed before. PCIT accounts for past trauma of both parent and child (unlike other methods that don't specifically acknowledge that parents have their own issues as well). PCIT helps the parent guide their child to lead during play, while still feeling comforted by the parental presence, rather than fearful or indifferent.

With this therapy, no assumptions or judgments are made about parenting skills. You won't be made to feel bad if you struggle to help your child regulate their emotions. Unburdened by this perspective, you can lower your guard and be honest about what life is like with your child. The practitioner is there to sit with you through your pain of not being able to help your child succeed. In the moments when you do make mistakes, they help you be a better parent. This therapy succeeds in supporting parents in their most vulnerable moments.

Medications

Medicating your child is usually one of the most difficult decisions a parent can make. Often the choice involves knowing the treatment may really help your child, but could also make your child's life more difficult.

When having all the necessary, and sometimes fraught, conversations about side effects, risk factors, and benefits, remember medications do help kids with Asperger's in ways that therapy, parenting classes, education, and time never will. Put simply, medications work.

I know many parents who have decided to use medications and have seen great results. Whenever parents tell me their child's twice-daily tantrums are now two times a week, I can hear the relief in their voice. Their child is able to connect more with peers, tolerate a board game, and, most important, be more themselves. Medications cannot cure autism, but they can help decrease the intensity of the symptoms.

At the same time, I also know some parents who have not experienced improvements or positive results from medication. When consulting with your doctor, remember the choice is ultimately yours. Most psychiatrists will start with a really low dose to mitigate the side effects.

There are three common medication types recommended for ASD and autism-related behavioral problems:

Anti-anxiety medications are often prescribed for individuals with Asperger's who have excessive worries or really struggle with intrusive thoughts and obsessive-compulsive behavior. If a child's worries are incredibly intense, managing most of their life is very difficult for them. They may feel like people are always watching and judging them. I've seen many kids, some with severe anxiety, take anti-anxiety medications like Lexapro and be able to tolerate going into a school environment.

Antidepressant medications often help with the hopelessness so many children with Asperger's feel, especially teenagers. Seeing teenagers with Asperger's having thoughts of suicide or wanting to escape this world or even making suicide attempts is tragically common. The rate of suicidal ideation among these kids is higher than the general population. (In some cases, language difficulties may contribute. For example, many of the teenagers I've helped have found it difficult to articulate that they feel overwhelmed and state instead that they want to kill themselves.) These medications are intended to decrease the intensity of such thoughts, helping the child stay in the present and feel less overwhelmed by the world. Their problems don't vanish, but they gain more energy to be brave.

Anti-aggressive (aka antipsychotic) medications aren't pre-scribed for individuals with Asperger's to treat psychosis, but to reduce aggressive behavior. Children with Asperger's can have intense behaviors that lead them to be aggressive with their parents, siblings, and care providers. These medications decrease the intensity of those meltdowns and shorten their time span. Less acting out increases the child's self-esteem, improves their chances of not being expelled from school, and helps them get along better with their parents. Risperidone (Risperidal) is the most commonly prescribed medication for this purpose.

Medication should work in concert with, not in place of, other treatment methods. The goal is to decrease the intensity of nega-tive behaviors, depression, or anxiety. A psychiatrist and therapist often work together to prescribe a medication while doing CBT. The medication helps decrease the intensity of the child's worries or thoughts to a manageable level, giving the therapy time to work and allowing the child to be eased off the medication. Most people with Asperger's are able to discontinue medication eventually, though there's no shame in needing to continue.

WHAT ABOUT DIET?

Many diet recommendations abound for children on the spectrum, and not all are credible. The most important priority is for your child to have a healthy, nutritionally sound diet. Many aspie kids have food sensitivities, so it can be challenging to make sure they eat healthy. Consult with your family doctor and, if needed, a dietician.

The most common dietary change associated with ASD is the gluten-free casein-free diet (GFCF). In 2008, when this way of eating was most popular, I heard from many parents that eliminating these foods from their child's diet was very successful—and took a lot of work to follow. A few studies have demonstrated the GFCF diet had no significant impact on children's behavior; a few others, such as the 2017 study by Piwowarczyk et al., have suggested that doing so is helpful for children with food sensitivities or gut issues.

A growing consensus charges that gut bacteria plays a role in the development of autism. For the hyperactive child on the spectrum, quite a few studies recommend that children not ingest foods with food coloring because of an association with increased hyperactivity. Dietary intervention is among the most controversial areas of treating autism. Until a consistently successful diet is established, I suggest checking in with the Eunice Kennedy Shriver National Institute of Child Health and Human Development about autism treatments (NICHD.NIH.gov), and making an informed decision.

What to Expect from This Book

Now that you have a general understanding of Asperger's, the most popular treatments, and how the condition impacts your child and family, let's roll up our sleeves and start making the changes that will empower your neurodiverse child to thrive. Going forward, each chapter is broken into specific strategies and actions you can use at home, at school, or in the community to help your child succeed. This book is designed for you, the parent. So, as you read through the rest of the book, take notes, decide which ideas have the most relevance for you, and try them out to see if they work. Highlight the advice that's helpful, make changes to fit your needs, and keep going! Keep doing what works.

Remember that as your neurodiverse child goes through a process of diagnosis—understanding what having the condition means and learning how to navigate in a neurotypical world—you are going through a very similar journey. At times, you will feel overwhelmed with the decisions you have to make, intimidated by potential side effects of treatments you're considering, or isolated from other parents and families who don't understand your situation. Turn to this book to remind yourself that difficult days are part of the process and you're not alone.

There's more to parenting an aspie kid than managing meltdowns and meeting with teachers. In the following chapters, I provide strategies that will have you excited to drop your child off for an amazing day at school, rather than relieved you'll have a break. And your whole family will benefit from a home life that's unique and rewarding and not centered around crisis management. Parenting a first-grader is significantly different from parenting a tenth-grader, so we'll touch on major milestones for different age groups and how to adapt the tools as your child improves and grows older.

This is also the beginning of your family's journey toward peace and a sense of pride in your child. You get to celebrate their areas of interest instead of being frustrated by them. When they spend more much time on the computer than you'd like, you'll be better at tolerating their behavior. You'll look forward to your neurodi-verse child having a great time hanging out with their neurotypical friend, because your kid is empowered with strategies and tips to get them through any social rough spots.

We'll begin this stage of our journey with some strategies to be a meaningful and effective parent: at home, school, and with friends and family. The next chapter also prioritizes self-care, so you can be more yourself, rather than a parent who's constantly worried about what their child will do next.

3

To Be a Meaningful Parent

Meaningfully parenting a child with Asperger's is an ongoing balancing act. There's the need to protect your child from people who just don't understand them. But there's also the need to urge your child to slowly move beyond their comfort zone, without shame and without excessive fear. Parents must prioritize helping their child grow in a direction of the child's choosing.

A resilient child is a happy child. Raising a child who can bravely face the challenges of life may be, in the end, the most meaningful act of parenting one can accomplish.

Seek Support

With a clearer picture of your child's needs, your next challenge is figuring out how to support your neurodiverse child while maintaining your own well-being. Always remember, your mental health as a parent is the most necessary component of your journey with your child. Both of you will benefit if you seek support from others to keep you buoyed in rough waters.

Finding the right kind of support is a personal preference. You might look to a formal parent support group, trusted friends, a religious-affiliated group, or other parents who you befriend at the park, school, or at the doctor's office—or all of the above. What matters is that you have others you can open up with to help you dissipate the intense emotions you feel. As you build a network, here are some points to keep in mind:

Common ground is comforting. When you cope with your emotions about your child's diagnosis by connecting with other parents in a similar situation, you'll find peace and acceptance.

Therapy helps. If you're feeling overwhelmed, there's no shame in seeking a therapist for support. Doing so means you want to be healthy and use the tools and resources someone trained in mental health care can provide so you can navigate your family's journey.

Find support for your child as well. Try getting your child in a group that teaches skills for interacting with neurotypical friends or getting them involved in school or hobby groups that relate to their interests. Many of the teens I've treated tend to resist Asperger's-specific groups, but if adults allow them to lead the group they seem to come around.

Share resources. If you are a parent of a young child, consider trading off babysitting with parents of children who have a similar diagnosis. One couple can have a date night, and their child can have some fun socialization with a family who understands them—a win-win for everyone.

Dive into discussions. You will likely purchase many books about Asperger's beyond this one, read articles and interviews, watch videos, and do other research. Your support network offers an opportunity to discuss, formulate a perspective, and compare your thoughts with other parents and professionals.

Share the burden. All parents of children with ASD want to protect their children from the negative effects of this diagnosis. But the painful reality is that it isn't always possible to do so. Sharing your experiences with others helps the pain dissipate, and seeing other families who have been dealing with this condition for a while gives you hope that life gets better.

FIND YOUR PEOPLE

One of the best ways parents can help themselves and their child is to find a local support group for families with an ASD diagnosis. In fact, I always encourage my clients to take this step as soon as possible. I can't express how important it is to find others going through similar experiences in order to understand and embrace your newfound world.

These groups are excellent resources for the latest research, local events, and for meeting other families and planning playdates for the younger kids. Think of these groups as a source of knowledge to help you and your family get up to speed, and as a safe space to share your concerns. Inevitably, you'll receive advice from someone who's been through a similar trial. Many of the mothers I help in my practice talk about their "mom village" as their main source of comfort, resources, and feedback. In my experience, these groups tend not to include many fathers. If you're a father participating in a support group, be proud you're defying the stereotype.

GET INVOLVED

Currently, three prominent patient associations have large followings in the United States:

Asperger / Autism Network (AANE): This group is oriented toward individuals and families diagnosed with autism and Asperger's, and it prioritizes the goals of the individual diagnosed. Their priority is to provide a non-judgmental space and work against misperception. AANE.org

The Autism Community in Action (TACA): This group's main focus is seeking out treatments and parental support for families affected by autism. Formerly known as "Talk about Curing Autism," the group has raised significant funds for autism research and advocacy. TACANOW.org.

Autism Speaks: This group funds research projects and treatments and offers support groups and resources. They have been criticized for not paying attention to the needs or voices of those diagnosed with autism and focusing on parents instead. But in 2020, the group made significant efforts to be more inclusive of individuals diagnosed with autism. AutismSpeaks.org.

YOU'RE NOT ALONE

How common is a diagnosis of Asperger's? While specific statistics are no longer kept for the total number of Asperger's cases diagnosed each year, as of 2016, 1 in 54 children in the United States was diagnosed with an ASD (including Asperger's cases). According to a conservative estimate by the Asperger / Autism Network, 1 in 500 children is diagnosed with Asperger's. Considering there are 100 million children in the United States, this ratio works out to be at least 200,000 cases. In 2015, the Global Burden of Disease Study stated 37 million individuals worldwide have been diagnosed with Asperger's, which works out to roughly 1 in 200 children.

Stay Educated

Finding out your child has Asperger's can be exhausting and discouraging. You may feel overwhelmed by the amount of information to take in. But the more you learn about this condition, the more you'll enhance your understanding of your child's challenges and perspective. Educating yourself builds hope, decreases irrational fears, and improves your understanding of your child's condition. You can learn more about Asperger's from a variety of sources—research articles, books, blogs, YouTube videos, even pop culture references, movies, TV shows, and anime—which can improve your understanding of neurodiversity.

For example, Alex Olinkiewicz's "In My Mind" video about Asperger's describes what the world is like from his perspective (see References, page 156). Steve Silberman's book *Neurotribes* is a mind-expanding look at how, when we flock together based on our interests, we are able to feel accepted. Learning more, instead of avoiding the sometimes difficult realities of life with a neurodiverse child, makes life more fulfilling.

The best ways to get educated are to join support groups, take parenting classes, and, most important, be open to changing your mind. Facts and statistics about Asperger's are one thing; when you truly learn and understand the nuanced differences between individuals with Asperger's and neurotypical individuals, your child's uniqueness begins to make more sense.

TAKE PARENTING CLASSES

Parenting classes are an undervalued asset in helping your child succeed. Improving your parenting style means you're adapting to your child's growth, not correcting your bad parenting habits. And that's all the more true with a neurodiverse child, as your neurotypical intuition won't always serve you well. Don't get me wrong: Most parents of a child with Asperger's only have to tweak their parenting style to be successful. But that small step can have a big impact and can take some seriously creative problem-solving to understand neurodiverse kids.

Fortunately, when we turn to the science of parenting, we can find pretty good instructions. The Incredible Years (Incredible-Years.com) has a solid program that teaches parents of four- to eight-year-olds emotional regulation skills and has a classroom component for teachers. The Kazdin method (AlanKazdin.com) is a parent training class created by a Yale University professor of child psychiatry. The emphasis is on investigating unhealthy behavior, figuring out your child's unmet needs, and offering the opposite of the negative behavior. The website claims to have an 80 percent success rate. The Collaborative Problem Solving Parenting method, mentioned in the last chapter (see page 31), helps reframe negative behavior as a lagging skill rather than a strong will. I also recommend *Your Defiant Child*, a book by child psychologist Russell A. Barkley, PhD (see References, page 156).

RETHINK HOW YOU COMMUNICATE

Changing the way you communicate with your child is no easy task and takes lots of practice and impulse control. Success depends on slowing down, recognizing the assumptions you're making in your language, and finding ways that make sense to communicate those assumptions to the neurodiverse point of view. Doing so might mean presenting information visually instead of verbally, such as in a chart that breaks down all the steps for doing chores. Or you may need to allow your child to do something other than look directly at you while you talk, to increase their chances of understanding what you're saying. This behavior doesn't make sense from a neurotypical point of view, but to the aspie child, it makes perfect sense. We'll explore communication issues in more detail in chapter 4 (see page 71).

PRACTICE RADICAL ACCEPTANCE

Let's be honest: Finding out your child has a disorder is angering, saddening, and frustrating. This diagnosis is not what you wanted for your child or what you envisioned for yourself as a parent. One way to deal with the intense emotions and discomfort that come with such an unwanted truth is to practice *radical acceptance*. This means accepting reality on reality's terms. To do so, we have to just be present in the moment, allowing things to be as they are without judging. Fighting reality is like trying to paint a waterfall: Your efforts will not last. Prioritizing acceptance and being present in your truth leads to long-term peacefulness.

Embrace the Positive

An Asperger's profile gives your child the ability to embrace a topic with passion. Your child will likely be incredibly honest, have a great memory, do well in school, be able to see things others wouldn't, and have perseverance to be admired.

When we are able to celebrate the strengths of Asperger's and accommodate for the challenges, a child's life can be amazing. So let's take a closer look at some of the specific advantages often associated with having Asperger's. While not every neurodiverse child will have all these strengths, they're more common in individuals with Asperger's than among neurotypical children.

Academic Excellence: The oft-repeated notion that young children with Asperger's are little professors rings true for many. Commonly, aspies are able to recite facts and knowledge in a monologue that will fascinate you; their cognitive ability is typically well beyond the average child's their same age. Asperger's often means a child's brain really gets excited to learn more information (if mostly in their areas of interest). For many kids, this academic interest usually leads to academic excellence and will help them succeed in school and life.

Superior Memory: Ask a child with Asperger's what you were just speaking about, and chances are they'll remember the bulk of the conversation, even if they didn't seem to be paying any attention. Many aspies have a superior ability to remember information and can easily recall data that would make most neurotypical students' heads spin. People who have Asperger's do much better than the general population when trying to recall specific facts or seemingly irrelevant trivia.

Visual Acuity: Many individuals on the spectrum have great visual discerning abilities, especially visual acuity. They can notice differences others cannot. Some studies have documented this claim, while others have debunked it. But most professionals who work with people who have Asperger's will agree that neurodiverse individuals seem to have overly perceptive senses (and some underdeveloped senses).

Rule Following: Nearly every child I've encountered who's diagnosed with ASD follows rules intensely. Kids with Asperger's are invested in doing things the right way, no matter what. This tendency really helps with doing schoolwork or completing a project. Neurodiverse people also follow rules they create for themselves, precepts they then use to break society's rules without guilt (often because they think society's rules are stupid). Though sometimes problematic, overall this approach is a strength. Being overly honest and following the rules usually leads to more success than failure. If I ever had to trust a person to come through for me, I would invariably choose someone with an Asperger's profile. They are exceptionally loyal and noble—a disposition I really admire.

Strong Convictions: Intense attachment toward beliefs is very common among aspies. Their convictions may sometimes come across as stubbornness but are typically paired with a drive to be honest and do what is right—much more so, generally speaking, than in their neurotypical peers. This quality can be a powerful motivator when pursuing a goal, though it can also push away a friend over an otherwise minor conflict. Perhaps the most famous example of a person with Asperger's following strong convictions is climate activist Greta Thunberg, whose vocal advocacy for carbon neutrality has attracted worldwide attention.

ASPERGER'S IN THE SPOTLIGHT

Over the past 25 years or so, Asperger's has become increasingly visible to the general public. With the condition becoming more familiar, a number of famous individuals, notable businesspeople, and celebrities have come forward to reveal their struggles with Asperger's. Parents can find relief knowing the diagnosis doesn't limit their child's potential for success. And your child might be heartened to know that a famous person, perhaps someone they admire or would enjoy learning about, shares their diagnosis. Examples include:

★ Ben Askren, successful mixed martial artist

★ Susan Boyle, singer and *American Idol* competitor

★ Temple Grandin, author, animal behavior scientist, autism activist

★ Bill Gross, CEO, Pacific Investment Management Company

★ Heather Kuzmich, fashion model

★ Daryl Hannah, actor (*Blade Runner, Splash, Steel Magnolias*)

★ Clay Marzo, competitive surfer

★ John Elder Robison, author and autism activist

★ Satoshi Tajiri, video game designer, creator of Pokémon

When discussing public figures who have Asperger's, be sure your information is accurate. Famous names from Albert Einstein to Bill Gates to Mark Zuckerberg have all been questionably linked to Asperger's without any disclosure or record of a diagnosis. Your child will research your reference.

Be Transparent with Your Child

How and when should you disclose to your child they have Asperger's? Virtually all parents stress over this question. True, the moment is important, but the conversation doesn't need to be overly serious or intense.

Here are a few tips to keep in mind when deciding how to discuss the diagnosis with your child:

Wait until after the evaluation. If you discuss the possibility of Asperger's beforehand, you may worry them for nothing or end up having to explain a completely different diagnosis. If they have questions about the testing, you can explain they are being evaluated for a few things, Asperger's being one of them.

Start with a small bit of information and gauge their reaction. Go slow and answer questions. Flooding any child with information can be stressful for them.

Explain they were born this way, and there was nothing they did to cause the condition. But now your whole family's responsibility is to understand what the diagnosis means and do their best to adapt.

Recognize your child's developmental level and use language they understand. Check in frequently to see how much they understand of what you're saying.

For a young child, I suggest sharing a narrative along these lines: We went to the doctor, and the doctor found you have something called Asperger's. This means understanding other people and having them understand you is harder for you. And, sometimes, doing something mommy and daddy ask of you is harder for you than for other kids. Now we have a way of understanding why.

For an older child, who likely knew they were having some type of evaluation, I suggest emphasizing their life isn't going to be worse because of the diagnosis. Instead, you'll all be aware there's a reason for the challenges they've been facing. Thanks to the diagnosis, you know their difficulties are not their fault.

Most important, be honest with your child, and don't dismiss or minimize the condition. Many children find knowing there's an explanation for the difficulties they've been having to be a relief. As a parent, you can highlight the positive aspects of the profile, especially highlighting the different, rather than the disability, angle. Their brain sees things in a unique and very useful way. They are able to sense things in a deeper way than most people can, and, more important, they are able to feel intense emotions in a way most neurotypicals envy.

Focus on Your Entire Family

Asperger's affects your entire life. Sometimes the presence of the condition is minimal; other times, debilitating. Coping strategies can be as simple as making sure you buy the same exact breakfast cereal for your child every time to prevent a meltdown. Or as complicated as spending months trying to figure out why your child avoids showering as if doing so were torture.

At either extreme, and in between, you'll have times that feel like Asperger's is taking over your entire family. This situation does not have to be the case: Asperger's should be just one aspect of your family's life. Let's discuss some ways parents can run a home with the family, not Asperger's, front and center.

GIVE YOUR PARTNER ATTENTION

There's no denying that having a child on the spectrum takes away from the time couples have to spend with each other. You and your partner may find yourselves always talking about ways to improve your child's life while neglecting conversations about enhancing your own relationship. You may feel guilty if you prioritize yourselves. In many cases, one parent becomes the child's intense advocate, while the other disconnects, becoming a distant observer.

When there's a child with Asperger's in the family, making time for your marriage or partnership isn't easy. But the importance of doing so can't be overstated. Here are some practices to help you make the most of the time available to you:

Plan intimate moments. Schedule a small window of 10 to 15 minutes each day to talk to each other about intimacy, love, and passion or to simply have some quiet time together, share a cup of coffee, or take a walk around the block.

Communicate all day. Write each other appreciative love notes and leave them where the other will find them while you're apart. Send short, cute text messages throughout the day.

Take a break. If you can arrange a childcare respite, take advantage of the time away for at least three hours per week. Go out on a proper date night. Feeling relief at being out in public without the kids is okay; parents of neurotypical children get excited about it all the time.

Give yourself permission. Placing your marriage above your child's needs is okay. To sustain the energy to take care of your child, you need to recharge your own battery and have fun occasionally without responsibility.

SPEND TIME WITH YOUR OTHER KIDS

One of the hardest things to do as a parent of a child who has Asperger's is avoid prioritizing them over your other children. Nurturing all your children is important, for their successes, uniqueness, and love. And while we expect our neurotypical kids to be caring and patient with their neurodiverse sibling—and they often are—we also need to recognize the compromises they make and give them a break. Their one-on-one time with you, and the connection you build with each other, will help them accept their sibling is coping with an inborn difference that really frustrates them and that they wish didn't get in the way so much.

Here are some suggestions to help neurotypical children grow into successful, confident adults:

Use your words. Be sure to share something you appreciate about them every single time you interact. Point out their kind words, diligence with chores, or a school achievement. Remind them they matter.

Go one-on-one. Schedule time with them apart from your aspie child. They likely change a bit so they don't offend your neurodiverse child, so you'll get a new window into their personality.

Support their interests. Enroll them in activities they request and get them there even if doing so is challenging. The saddest family compromises are when we ask a child to take one for the team.

Create rituals. Have a routine that includes something just for the two of you. Choose something as simple as a Saturday morning drive to Starbucks for hot chocolate.

ENCOURAGE SIBLING RELATIONSHIPS

Never doubt the value of managing the interactions between neurotypical children and aspie siblings. It's crucial that they connect with and understand one another so that resentment does not develop. If the relationship isn't nurtured, the neurotypical child can feel like their sibling is rejecting them or treating them negatively when they avoid social interactions or ruin an outing by melting down. And an aspie child can become quite overwhelmed by the behaviors of their neurotypical siblings.

Here are some steps to take to encourage a healthy, respectful relationship among siblings:

Schedule family time around the limitations or struggles your aspie child will face. No board games (both neurotypical and neurodiverse kids can take these too seriously), no competition—just fun absurd silliness everyone enjoys. Go swimming, goof around in the backyard, cook together, talk about your week.

Establish rules and routines around the house that will decrease your neurodiverse child's stress by providing predictability, especially around hygiene and cleanup time. If everyone has a designated time for, say, using the bathroom in the morning, fewer conflicts will arise.

Meet weekly as a family to discuss issues that may be brewing. When each person takes their turn to speak, require them to summarize what the other person has said, including as much emotional content as possible. We're usually less angry at the people who validate us.

You'll find other ways to promote harmony, all of which fall under the concept of "seek to understand above all else." For example, if the behavior of someone else angers your child, encourage this child to express to the other person what made them mad. Encourage the angry child to ask the other person why they behaved in the way they did, rather than assume the other person purposefully tried to hurt their feelings. This approach helps children learn that most incidents that make them angry are just misunderstandings, especially when a neurotypical person and neurodiverse person disagree.

The most challenging discussions with your neurotypical children, especially when they're young, are when you have to ask them to show understanding and compassion to their neurodiverse sibling. But the tools and practices outlined in this section will help your neurotypical kid feel heard and understood.

LOOP IN EXTENDED FAMILY AND FRIENDS

Whenever you're surrounded by a caring and understanding circle of friends and family, you feel a lot less overwhelmed by life's challenges, Asperger's included. For this reason, I recommend disclosing the diagnosis to people close to you (see "Parents and Family Relationships," page 21). But you may face some rough patches as you share the details. Here are some points to remember:

More info might help. Sometimes family members or friends who aren't familiar with Asperger's might dismiss the diagnosis, saying the child is just going through a phase, or write off your concerns altogether. In those cases, rather than defend your position, ask them if they would like to learn more about the diagnosis. I suggest directing them to AANE, TACA, Autism Speaks, and local church chapters dedicated to Autism and Asperger's.

Some people don't understand. Grandparents and extended family who haven't witnessed your child's struggles can have a hard time understanding the nuances of the disorder. I suggest first telling the family members who will likely understand and be supportive. As you build up the emotional momentum, it becomes easier to share with those who may find the diagnosis harder to accept.

It's up to you to end the conversation. In some cases, sharing details from the report with the diagnosis may help with those who resist the facts. But when someone rejects the diagnosis no matter what, let go of trying to convince them. And if their beliefs lead to negative consequences when they interact with your child, limiting their contact is best. The last thing you want is for your child to feel ashamed for being who they are.

Remember the upside. If informing someone about the diagnosis leads to a disappointing exchange, keep in mind those close to you who've offered acceptance and support. When your child is surrounded by people who understand and offer patience and empathy, they thrive. The more such a community surrounds your child, the more the child feels proud of who they are, goes beyond their comfort zone, and enjoys life.

MAKE TIME FOR YOURSELF

What's the difference between self-care and being selfish? If you struggle to answer this question, join the club. So many parents, especially mothers, make every effort to avoid being selfish and so neglect their own needs to take care of their child. The challenges and burdens of raising a child with Asperger's can exacerbate this instinct.

But what you don't often see when you skip lunch or stay up all night researching Asperger's support groups on the Internet is the toll you pay whenever you neglect yourself, neglect your needs, neglect your marriage, neglect your career, and neglect your health. Prioritizing these things, even if doing so means postponing some childcare tasks—you'll get to them—means you increase your resilience. And this prioritization of yourself is what enables you to be there for your child over the long haul.

Here are some principles to follow that will help you take better care of yourself so you can take care of your child:

Pay attention to your thoughts. Are you calling yourself names and criticizing yourself? Try talking to yourself the way you would to a close friend who's having a difficult time. Keep your self-talk honest, empathetic, supportive, and judgment-free.

Pay attention to your body. Look for signs your physical health is not okay—fatigue, headaches, stomach upset, muscle pain, or anything that indicates stress or illness—and take care of the problem. Get a massage, do yoga, get to a doctor, go for a run, or just do nothing to give yourself time to recharge.

Pay attention to your friends. Whenever you nurture your friendships, your friends nurture you. Whenever you excessively rely on your friends, they start disappearing. Be sure to spend time with people who are important to you, and when you do, make a point to discuss what's going on in *their* lives as well. And if a friend starts distancing from you, don't assume they're being selfish. Often this distance means they're overwhelmed and doing their own self-care. You may want to ask how they're doing.

Pay attention to your relationship. A good date night can do wonders for your marriage. Spending some time with your partner without having to take care of your kids recharges your batteries and reminds you why you're together in the first place.

Pay attention to your emotions. Being the parent of a child with Asperger's requires psychological flexibility. That's because your child may often be inflexible and have difficulty clearly communicating with you. Acceptance and Commitment Therapy can help in these situations. It teaches you how to be present in the moment with your child and observe the dilemma from an emotional distance. That same advice is also is useful when speaking with a teacher or your spouse about a difficult issue regarding your child. Don't let your thoughts rule your emotions. Pursue your values through committed action, even if the request feels painful to advocate for; it means you're accepting that your child is having difficulties and learning what works best for them. For more information on Acceptance and Commitment Therapy, please visit stevenchayes.com for a toolkit and resources. I highly recommend his latest work, *A Liberated Mind*.

ASPERGER'S AND DIVORCE

Having a child on the spectrum means doing everything you can for them will take up much of your energy, time, and sometimes hope. You will likely spend much less time than you want being relaxed and having fun, and more time with an ABA therapist at your house, or you'll feel like the chauffeur delivering your child to one appointment after another. Some days, just being in the same room at the same time as your partner will feel like an incredible achievement.

The good news is couples with a child who has Asperger's do not have a higher risk of divorce. The largest study on this topic found 64 percent of children on the spectrum have both parents at home, while 65 percent of neurotypical children have both parents living together. Nevertheless, an unnurtured relationship is unfulfilling and lonely, even if there is a great reason for neglecting the bond. Spend time with your partner, talk about your hopes and fears, and the two of you will thrive through this.

Learn to Advocate

My advice to parents of a neurodiverse child always includes this: Be brave, be confident, and be you. And if you don't think of yourself as an assertive person, don't worry. I've seen many parents transform from being shy and reserved into bold, confident people who will not take no for an answer from anyone who doesn't prioritize their child's needs.

Having a child with Asperger's means being misunderstood by most professionals, school districts, service coordinators, and others who you need on your side. The question is, "How do I stick up for my child without having to be a jerk?"

Here are some ways to strategically advocate for your child:

Challenge assumptions. When someone says your child will "just grow out of their behaviors," have them explore the consequences of being wrong versus right. Which outcome is more damaging? An exploratory conversation in which they take a turn considering what your child needs is the least conflict-prone way to resolve your differences.

Think collaboratively. Try to understand the position of decision-makers. Ask them to explain their reasoning, empathize with them, and build upon your shared goals to form a partnership.

Hire a pro. When arranging an IEP (individualized educational plan; see page 23) meeting, consider hiring an educational attorney. Laws and school district protocol can be incredibly confusing. To save yourself time and headaches, allow a professional who has a good relationship with the school district to be your advocate.

Do your research. Know what you would like for your child before you go into any municipal or county agency or regional center meeting. Find out what services are available so you can make specific requests.

Plan for trouble. In high school, many kids with Asperger's threaten to harm other students who treat them poorly. Aspies often use extreme language when angry. Many find it hard to say they're frustrated, so it's not unusual for them to say they are going to kill themselves or someone else. In most schools, threatening language gets you expelled. Before your child has an incident, speak with school authorities and advocate for a response that doesn't trigger the school's no-tolerance policy.

Explore restorative justice options. Many children on the spectrum end up interfacing with law enforcement for unexpected reasons. Restorative justice programs teach children and adolescents how their behavior impacts others, rather than assigning them community service or putting them on probation for a crime or serious violation of school policies. Find out how this approach can be invoked in your community, in case your child ever ends up on the wrong side of the law.

PART TWO

STRATEGIES

FOR YOU AND

YOUR CHILD

4

Strategies for Home

Home sweet home? Finding peace as a family is difficult if your child is having a dramatic, wall-shaking tantrum once a day. But when your child is able to clearly communicate their emotions, your entire family dynamic will pivot away from calamity and toward calm. In this chapter, you'll learn that peacefulness is possible and how strategic reasoning and acceptance can get you there.

Creating a Safe and Peaceful Home

Kids want their home to feel safe and peaceful. You probably do, too. Creating this kind of home life for a child with Asperger's depends on these two principles:

- **Understanding your kid's strengths** and doing your best to enhance them.
- **Understanding the challenges your kid faces** and doing your best not to make your child feel ashamed about them.

To truly abide by these principles, you'll have to apply them to yourself as well. We all need to improve our skills, and we all need to be able to seek help without being ashamed.

Neurodiverse kids can be really difficult to figure out. The first thing they need is safety and security. Their definition of these needs and the neurotypical definition of their needs isn't the same, so you have to enter their world.

Simply put: Have your kid define what safety means to them. Ask them to tell you, and please don't interrupt while they do. Be patient and write down what they say. This is your starting point. Use the techniques detailed throughout the rest of this chapter to keep the conversation going and create the safe, peaceful home environment that will benefit your whole family. And as you do, you'll find your way around the wall your child with Asperger's has put up between you. You will discover many new things about your child that will help you appreciate their perspective and point of view. Your child will see you believe in them, you trust them, and will defend them.

Guiding Theme: Communicate Clearly with Your Child

It can be unnerving to attempt to communicate with someone who's liable to start yelling. Kids with Asperger's often have an internal or external meltdown if they interpret what you say in an extreme light. To avoid this reaction, validate what the child is saying, then communicate the four Ws: who, what, when, and where. (Asking "Why?" usually leads to a conflict and rarely leads to a solution.) Here are a few examples.

For a preschooler: Be patient, and wait for them to stop being engrossed in whatever activity they're doing.

Start by connecting with your own emotions—know how you're feeling in this moment—and then making eye contact and possibly touching their arm. Next state specifically the who, what, when, and where of your need.

Example: "Jenny, I saw you had a lot of fun playing with your L.O.L. dolls. I need you to take them into your room and put them to bed in their storage box."

For a middle schooler: Be consistent in your message. If you change what you say or lie, they won't care whether you're clearly communicating.

Highlight the emotion you would like for them to feel, then use the four W's.

Example: "Hi Jenny, I would like for you to feel a little less over-whelmed. Please organize your desk by stacking your books on the bookshelf and putting the clothes hanging on your chair away in the closet before you get started on your homework. I'm here to help at any point."

For your high schooler: Remind them of their independence and your role as an advisor before giving a command. Begin with the end in mind.

Example: "Hi Jenny, do you have five minutes? I would like to check in with you about something but I know there is a lot on your plate." If she agrees, proceed; if not, schedule some time. When she is ready: "Hi Jenny, I know you're really responsible, but would you mind sitting with me as I go through the school's online parent portal so we can go over how school is going for you?"

UNDERSTAND EYE CONTACT

Almost all parents ask me about eye contact. If their neurodiverse child doesn't make eye contact with them in a conversation, they often wonder whether the child was paying attention. But don't mistake no eye contact for lack of interest. Many kids who have been diagnosed with Asperger's tell me that eye contact with others overwhelms them. They remember less of what a person is saying when forced to make eye contact, because they study the person's eyes and facial features excessively. They look away so they can focus on understanding and communicating.

That said, eye contact is such an important norm for neuro-typical people that helping your child do so more often is worth the effort, but you need to get their agreement and respect their comfort level. In a sense, this means teaching them a "masking" behavior: learning to tolerate discomfort and seem more like a neurotypical person to have an easier time in the neurotypical world.

Here are a few recommendations:

Figure out what leads you to want eye contact. Most parents want their child to show others they are paying attention. Often this really means parents want their child to show they care about others. If a healthy conversation is the goal, eye contact may work against this possibility.

Consider emotion-based planning. Is there some other way you can experience what you want from eye contact? If you want to be proud of your child for hearing you, try basing your feelings of satisfaction on their completion of the task.

Stay positive. Remind your child often how much you love seeing their smile or their eyes. If you make maintaining eye contact a negative issue or they sense you're frustrated because they don't look at you, they will likely avoid eye contact more.

Be patient. If your child isn't listening to you and you need them to take care of a task such as cleaning their room or picking up their breakfast dishes, try this sequence. This strategy is best for kids in elementary school or younger. If you have a teen who needs some direction, you may need to be more stern because they—like all teens—aren't as malleable to parental influence as a younger child tends to be.

1. Before you begin, ask your child to face you. This may take a few minutes. Don't get discouraged, just gently ask your child to put down whatever they're doing and face you. Lightly touch their shoulder, if needed.

2. You may need to remove an item from their hands to get their attention.

3. Once they turn toward you, ask them to look at you. Again, this could take a few minutes and will require patience on your part.

4. Continue to say their name in a firm but gentle tone to encourage them to look up.

5. If after several minutes they have not complied, walk away and try again after about 20 minutes. Start by asking them what may have held them back last time.

CLEAR LANGUAGE IS BEST

An aspie child usually understands what you literally said—not what you meant, not what you implied, not what you expected them to get. So to communicate clearly, you have to speak their language. Doing so means using concise language without figurative speech or metaphors. And because they want the literal truth and nothing more, speaking to a child with Asperger's using theory, examples, and anecdotes tends to overwhelm them.

Even when you're as clear as you can be, often a neurodiverse child needs time to process what you've said. As you wait for a response, you may be tempted to assume they're distracted, avoiding the topic, or being rude. But more likely they're not quite ready to answer, and if you're patient, they'll reply. Don't try to speed up their thinking, which may provoke a meltdown. While you wait, remind yourself that communicating their way increases the chance of comprehension for both of you.

A QUICK REVIEW OF BEST PRACTICES

Here's a cheat sheet of principles that will help you communicate clearly with your neurodiverse child.

★ Slow down and explore their perspective. "So what you mean by what you said is . . ."

★ Validate that what they're saying is their truth. "I bet that's very frustrating for you."

★ Avoid giving metaphors and theory. "When I said 'I'm lost,' I just meant I don't know what to do about this problem."

★ Go step by step in your description of a task, without skipping anything. "Please pick your clothes up off the floor. Hang the jacket in the closet, put the socks and shirts in the hamper, and then put the hamper back in the corner."

★ Check for comprehension often. "Does what I said make sense? Do you have any questions before I continue?"

FACTS MATTER, NOT TONE

Neurodiverse children often just relate to the content of what you said, rather than such nonverbal communication cues like your tone of voice, body language, or gaze. Unlike neurotypical kids, children with Asperger's pay much more attention to facts than emotions when communicating.

But gaining a better understanding about tone of voice helps neurodiverse children interact with the neurotypical world. If your child tends to misinterpret most tones as negative, validate their frustration rather than telling them they're wrong. For example, if they say you're yelling, don't argue that you're not. Believe they heard yelling and speak extra softly.

A good method to help your child learn more about tone of voice is to watch a TV show with them and discuss how the characters are expressing emotions. A cartoon like *Spongebob Squarepants,* with exaggerated voices and heightened emotions, is usually a good choice. Be sure to joke around and keep this process fun, rather than formalizing what you're doing.

When a character on screen says something that relies on voice tone—a joke, a sarcastic comment, a vocalization like "Ah!" or "Wow!"—ask your child, "What do you think he means by having his voice sound that way?" If their response is incorrect, only offer your own interpretation in a calm, nonchalant manner. Over time, your child will realize they can train themselves to notice that tone of voice and the significance.

GIVE THEM AN ESCAPE HATCH OR PARACHUTE

For kids on the spectrum, going out into the world can feel like going into a war zone. Giving them an option to bail out of a difficult exchange instead of tolerating the distress can mean one less stressor in a difficult day. This strategy is simple: You and your child agree on a safety word ("parachute" is an easy choice), and when either of you invokes the word, the conversation ends. You're both allowed to exit the situation immediately and reconvene when you're both ready (or in a predetermined amount of time). This escape hatch makes going beyond their comfort zone easier because they'll tolerate difficult conversations knowing they can hit the brakes if things get really bad. Have them choose the word and then practice a few times with you.

Example: Your child is trying to do homework, and their pencil keeps breaking because they keep tapping the point on the table and breaking the graphite. You keep reminding them to not tap the pencil; they keep getting mad. They keep getting up to sharpen the pencil and you think they're procrastinating. If either of you feels like a blowup is about to happen, someone gets to say "Parachute!" You both take a 10-minute break to self-regulate without judgment. You then regroup and figure things out.

EMBRACE PRACTICE SCRIPTS

Kids on the spectrum do not have great prediction engines. The world surprises them. Practice scripts are great for decreasing your child's fear about an upcoming expectation. Here's an example of motivating your preteen child with a quick practice script:

Dad: Hey Aiden, I know you haven't been to this restaurant we're going to tomorrow. Would you like to practice how to speak with the waiter?

Aiden: No.

Dad: I get that you don't want to have to think about things that make you upset until you have to deal with them.

Aiden: Yep.

Dad: What if I told you that if we rehearse ahead of time, we'd just be practicing, so you wouldn't have to continue the conversation if anything gets frustrating. Remember last time we didn't know what you wanted to eat, you got really upset and then didn't eat anything? You had a big meltdown when the food arrived and you left the restaurant hungry.

Aiden: Let's get this over with.

Dad: I am Aiden, you are the waiter, sound good?

Aiden: This is painful. What would you like for dinner, little dude?

Dad: I have some sensitivities to wheat and dairy, and strawberries are terrible. What would you recommend?

Aiden: I can do that? Umm ... I will check with the manager and come right back.

Dad: Sounds great. Thank you.

Aiden: Don't tell anyone I told you this, but this practice may actually help.

Note that the example dad did not get frustrated with Aiden's sarcasm or lack of enthusiasm. He addressed the child's unstated needs with a script that would put responsibility on the waiter to meet Aiden's restricted diet. This preempted Aiden's concern he'd be overwhelmed by looking at a menu. Whenever you come up with scripts for home life or school, keep past situations in mind and remind your child that getting comfortable with these interactions is a work in progress. I suggest that most kids keep a notebook of helpful scripts to refer to when needed.

Guiding Theme: Set Ground Rules

Many kids with Asperger's are amazing at following the rules, usually to a perfectionist, inflexible standard. Teens with Asperger's are surprisingly good at being deceptive whenever they do break rules—which they do because they have their own internal rules to follow. In that light, here are some tips for setting rules based on your neurodiverse child's age.

Elementary school children: I suggest parents stick to three basic rules for each situation that requires direction; more than three is overwhelming for a child with Asperger's. Also helpful is to give them a pass sometimes on less important rules to help them learn to self-regulate after a mistake.

Middle school kids: This age group is especially sensitive to negative feedback. Seventh and eighth grade can be a brutal period for kids on the spectrum. They already receive judgment every day at school; the last thing they need is for their parents to do the same. When something goes wrong, ask your child if they noticed things did not go well and then explore their perspective.

Teenagers on the spectrum: This age group will find the exception to your rules and may mistake your kindness as weakness if you're inconsistent with enforcement. For example, suppose your neurodiverse teenager has been frequently breaking a rule and denies doing so. Parenting 101 tells you to have a consequence for your teen's rule-breaking and dishonesty. But even after you issue a consequence, your child may continue to break that rule. They may just keep doing what they are doing and accept the inevitable consequence. Try changing the conversation from the consequences of not following what's asked of them to issues of loyalty, fidelity, and respect. You'll likely get more traction.

POSITIVE FEEDBACK

We are so often overloaded with just getting through the day we can forget to celebrate when things go well. Many kids on the spectrum are responsible, courteous, mature members of society. As a therapist, I sit on a tall metaphorical stack of research that states the more you, as the parent, consistently acknowledge this good behavior, the more good behavior you'll see. Here are a few examples to use with your middle schooler:

"I see you turned in everything on time today. You are so on top of things!"

"That was really cool of you to tell your friends on your own you had to get off *Minecraft* to eat dinner. Seeing you help out your sibling when no one was looking made my heart happy."

"I really appreciate when you tell me an honest reason why you can't get something done, rather than lie and say you already finished the work to avoid consequences."

POSITIVE DISCIPLINE

Neurodiverse kids make a lot of mistakes. Offering constructive advice and guiding them based on what they did right, instead of punishment, seems to help them recover faster and with long-term self-esteem intact. Here is an example of positive discipline at work:

> **Mom:** Hey Sasha, I'm confused about how you handled your sister asking you to play with her.
>
> **Sasha:** Yeah, me, too. I don't know what to do about her.
>
> **Mom:** Would you like some suggestions?
>
> **Sasha:** I'm not sure you're going to tell me anything new.
>
> **Mom:** It may help to schedule play time with her so she's not always bugging you and interrupting your deep thoughts. She would know you'll follow through during that scheduled time and respect your boundaries more.
>
> **Sasha:** This feels weird. Why are you not telling me to be patient with her? She is younger and I shouldn't shove anyone.
>
> **Mom:** It sounds like you already know what you should do. What good would reminding you do? I get you are sometimes flooded, and regaining your focus can take a while. Mistakes happen, then you learn from them and move on.

MAKE ROOM FOR FLEXIBILITY

As a parent of a strong-willed neurodiverse child, the last thing you need to do is assert your control. Doing so just creates a fight, and if your child concedes, her self-esteem is lowered. No matter the outcome, you both lose. Our goal is to teach our children with Asperger's to be confident and flexible. If we teach them the skill of flexibility by example, we're bound to succeed as well as solve the problem at hand. Double win!

In the following example, I will walk through how to discuss chores in an engaging and nonjudgmental way with your child.

Parent: I hear you say you won't clean up your room.

Child: Yeah, I like my room this way. I can find things.

Parent: Challenge accepted.

Child: What?

Parent: You said you can find things better, right? So please find all your socks.

Child: I can't find them. They may be under stuff or under my bed.

Parent: Exactly. Not being able to find clothes is what makes doing laundry difficult for me. Can we go on a sock hunt together?

Child: (rolls eyes) Sure . . .

Let go of needing your child to be normal. They're going to take a more unique path to adulthood, one that may frequently surprise you. They may not reason through things like you do, so follow their lead while helping them avoid pitfalls, rather than trying to get them to do things your way. Especially because there are several "right ways" to do most things.

THE IMPORTANCE OF HYGIENE

Many kids on the spectrum avoid their hygiene routine as often as possible. Reminding them how much they smell is usually not a motivator, nor is yelling at them that everyone has to do these tasks. The reasons behind this resistance typically aren't always clear, but here's my take: Usually, you can't logic them into improving. You are not going to convince a neurodiverse child about the benefits of washing or get them to change their behavior by explaining the social and health reasons for maintaining good hygiene. Instead, you'll need to become a detective, ask questions, be patient, and investigate step by step until you reach the root of the problem. One useful avenue to pursue is to ask about sensory issues. Some of the strategies I have seen work are:

- Changing out the showerhead to one that doesn't hurt their skin as much or won't make an annoying sound.
- Introducing them to liquid soap and a shower sponge if they feel uncomfortable using their hands to wash their body.

EMBRACING THEIR PASSIONS

"Hey Mom, did you know on *Pokémon Go*, if you rename Eevee to Rainer and evolve the character, it turns into Vaporeon?"

If that sentence make sense to you or you've heard a similar one, you understand. When your child loves something, they LOVE it. They know every detail you can imagine, whether it's Dungeons & Dragons, *Magic: The Gathering*, chess, or any other game guided by volumes of rules and strategy; a television or movie franchise; or a species of animal or period in history. I encourage you to hear your child out and keep reminding them you're so proud that they really love something.

Whenever kids on the spectrum feel rejected over their passions, their heart breaks. Keep their flame lit by asking about their passion regularly, rather than waiting for them to bring up the topic. And instead of trying to get them to limit their attempts to share, use these conversations to help them summarize what they want to say, so they can talk about what they love more easily with others.

Guiding Theme: Learn the Art of Defusing

You don't need me to tell you your neurodiverse child's emotions can be intense. Children with Asperger's often demand things to be their way, and if things do not go their way, they can spin into a tornado that might be very brief or go on all day. These incidents are difficult to predict, but there are ways to interrupt or defuse them. To start our survey of the art of defusion, here are three key strategies:

- **Distraction:** Sending their attention elsewhere is the simplest and easiest move to make, a go-to whenever you're feeling overloaded. When your child is in a meltdown over one specific topic, mention something completely unrelated that interests them. Their strong connection to the new subject may override their emotion.

- **Direct Address:** Speak directly about how difficult their behavior is for you. You might say, "I really want to hear you, what you're saying sounds really important, but you're speaking so loudly my ears can't hear you." This technique has a low success rate, but when it works, the result is magical.

- **Relocation:** If the blowout is related to the location you're in, your child may not be able to articulate how overwhelmed the environment is making them feel. Relocating—or just the act of walking—truly helps children self-regulate. If they're on the ground kicking and screaming or hitting you, start to walk away and often they will follow (if for no other reason than to keep hitting you).

HIT PAUSE

Sometimes our kids push our buttons and we don't know when to stop. We get so deep into an argument that we don't realize how dysregulated we are. In these situations, I recommend parents or their children use a pause or escape word (see "Give Them an Escape Hatch or Parachute," page 77) to take a 15-minute break and come back to the topic.

REMOVE YOUR CHILD FROM THE SITUATION

We can't help but feel like a tantrum or meltdown is a reflection on our own bad parenting. In reality, for kids with Asperger's, such behavior is usually a consequence of being overwhelmed or finding themselves in a situation without the skills to handle what they're experiencing. Removing them from the situation without blaming or shaming them allows the two of you to talk about what they can do differently next time. Here's a practice script that shows how to approach the situation:

Parent: Hey Bart, I see you were having a lot of fun outside with your friends and your engine is overheating; you may need a drink of water and to fix your shoelaces. Would you mind coming over here?

Child: No, I'm fine!

Parent: I hear you that you are fine, and you got this. Can you feel if your forehead is warm? (Most kids in the midst of a tantrum will feel warm.)

Child: Maybe?

Parent: Trust me, I want you to have fun, but we need to have a drink, cool down, and talk before we play again.

Child: I don't want to!

Parent: I know, and fighting your feelings is hard, huh?

Child: Yeah.

Parent: I love you.

Child: Love you, too (walking toward the parent).

It's okay to remove your child from a situation when they are over-whelmed or having an emotional outburst. And there is no need for either of you to feel shame or embarrassment in the process, or to give them any consequences.

THE PAPER FIGHT

This may be my favorite way to defuse. A child with Asperger's may take a long time to get their thoughts together and clearly express themselves, especially when upset during a disagreement. Using written communication levels the playing field. When experiencing a conflict, try encouraging your child to write down their thoughts and feelings about what's happened—a single paragraph is enough—on a sheet of paper. You do the same. Then exchange sheets and each of you write a response to the other's note. Repeat until both parties feel understood, even if the disagreement isn't resolved. This greatly decreases the chances of yelling at each other and greatly increases the chances of truly understanding each other. Having each others' points of view laid out in front of you really helps.

INDUCTIVE REASONING SKILLS

One of the reasons neurodiverse and neurotypical individuals have communication difficulties is they tend to use different types of reasoning.

Deductive reasoning is the type preferred by most aspies. This way of thinking relies on facts: If A is true, and B is true, then C must be true. Theories and general rules with exceptions are hard for neurodiverse people to follow, but facts are their friends.

Abductive reasoning is the process of finding the most likely explanation for something, even if there's no solid evidence for a conclusion. This is the type of thinking that is second nature to parents and most neurotypical adults. For example, "If the animal walks like a duck, swims like a duck, and quacks like a duck, it probably is a duck." Abductive reasoning means using intuition and past experience to decide on the best answer.

Fortunately, there's a middle ground—*inductive reasoning*—and the more you and your child use this route, the higher the likelihood you'll understand each other. With this approach, you blend your intuition with data to come to a reasonable conclusion. The typical process is:

1. Observing the facts.

2. Asking great questions about the facts.

3. Trusting you have a good enough answer about how to proceed.

THE LAW OF FIRSTS

Have you ever compared a repeat experience with the first time? Maybe you've gone back to a restaurant you enjoyed and found the same meal wasn't as great as you remember. Or you rewatched a movie you once hated and found that the story wasn't so bad after all. Your initial assessment may have seemed accurate, despite being too forgiving or too harsh, because of the "law of firsts"—the notion that the first impression someone has will influence the rest of their observations. Neurotypical individuals are able to adapt rather well if their first impression turns out to be inaccurate. But someone with Asperger's will struggle more with the concept. A bad initial experience may even trigger post-traumatic stress syndrome. And a great experience may lead a neurodiverse person to obsessively seek a repeat.

For someone with Asperger's, the intensity of such avoidance or pursuit does not realistically match what actually happened. Some kids turn into accidental stalkers if someone is nice to them or won't give somebody a second chance after a bad first meeting. Even in the face of evidence that the initial experience is no longer accurate or applicable, aspie kids nonetheless tend to consider the first impression to be the only possible outcome.

Overturn the law of firsts with these steps:

1. Work together to identify your child is being inflexible.

2. Ask your child if any evidence would convince them to change their mind. The more you can identify what would shift their assessment, the more likely your child will accept other possibilities.

3. Explore the strengths and weakness of their perspective, emphasizing facts.

4. Ask them if you can both figure out an alternative experience that could be as beneficial as the one they're avoiding or pursing.

5. Teach them there are many right answers to most problems, and having a toolbox full of solutions is great.

Example:

Parent: Hey Cameron, I know I gave you extra sugar on your cereal last week and you loved the taste, right?

Cameron: Yes, I want sugar on my cereal every time and when you don't let me, I get mad.

Parent: I know you want extra sugar every time, but that time was a special treat. I am not comfortable giving you extra sugar every morning.

Cameron: (exasperated sigh) I hate you.

Parent: I understand you are frustrated that you don't get to have things the same way as the first time. I would feel frustrated, too. Could you find a way to still be pretty happy with the cereal without sugar, just not super happy?

Cameron: No, I am not going to eat my cereal now. You ruined it!

Parent: I hear you say I ruined your cereal. Those words make me sad.

Cameron: Whatever.

Parent: You have a file in your brain with that bowl of cereal with the extra sugar. And if I try to tell you the cereal would be good without the sugar, your brain says, "But the cereal isn't the same," right?

Cameron: Kind of, yeah.

Parent: I feel for you.

Cameron: Thanks. Just give me something else.

Parent: OK.

5

Strategies for School

Neurodiverse children must learn to self-regulate their emotions to have any chance of succeeding intellectually, so social-emotional learning is key to their academic success. As we explore strategies for empowering your child to thrive at school, you'll see the importance of two key concepts: adapting to your child's challenges (learning a new skill to help them succeed) and accommodating your child's challenges (acknowledging a deficit and finding a work-around).

Setting Them Up for Success

Let's start this chapter by defining success. What would success at school look like for your child?

I once considered a measure of success to be the ability of a grade-schooler with Asperger's to tell me the name of another child in their class. I now realize that was a terrible measure! Often neurodiverse kids don't care about names. A more relevant measure is the ability of a child to tell me they had fun playing with someone at recess, which signals a decrease in their anxiety and an improvement in their communication. Chances are they recharged their emotional battery, which helped them be more flexible to get through the afternoon's classwork.

What will success look like for your neurodiverse child? Only you, working with the professionals involved in your child's education, can make this determination. As you think through the possibilities, follow these guidelines:

Tap into their passions. Your child's strongest interests make the best motivators. Let them take the lead on how they want to spend their time. Maybe they have a special interest in airplanes or robotics. Whatever their interest is, when you see your child's eyes light up about a topic, explore more. When they experience happiness and excitement, they are in a better mood with you and more likely to trust your parenting suggestions about other topics. Your child's success isn't defined by following society's rules, but by having a great time following your rules while completing a personally meaningful task.

Focus on their strengths. When developing your child's education plan, tailor it around their strengths rather than their challenges. For example, if a teenager struggles in reading but is very proud of their math ability, make sure the day's first class is math. I've seen many school administrators try to schedule a neurodiverse student's most challenging class first, thinking that's when the child will be at their strongest. But having that class first means the child is likely to resist going to school altogether.

Keep goals manageable. As you develop your plan to improve your child's academic success, make sure you only address one or two challenges at a time. With just a few goals to work toward, improvement is easier for them to notice.

Their Educational Rights

Every child in the United States has the right to a Free Appropriate Public Education (FAPE). This means if your child needs the school to adapt to make their education more appropriate, the school must do so, at no cost to you.

In my experience, school administrators really do want to help your child but are limited in what they can offer because of budget constraints. With that in mind, your approach should be to align with public school officials, rather than take an adversarial position, and work to convince them your child is worth the investment. As we delve into your options, be mindful of these points:

Delays are unacceptable. This area is one where I recommend inflexibility. Don't put up with arguments that "We should wait and see what happens" before the school makes accommodations. The longer a student is in an environment that doesn't support their learning style, the more likely they'll give up on the education system altogether.

Start with a 504. Whenever your child is first diagnosed, ask the evaluator about how to start developing a 504 plan. This refers to section 504 of the Rehabilitation Act of 1973 and is applicable anywhere in the United States. If a 504 plan doesn't cover your child's needs, request an Individualized Education Plan (IEP). This process includes an opportunity to assess your child more thoroughly, and arrange more intense interventions such as a classroom aide or a special day class. I'll get into more detail about 504s and IEPs in the section titled "IEP versus 504" on page 95.

Help is available. Navigating this maze of options and resources is almost always challenging, and federal funding opportunities are available for all parents to learn about the Individuals with Disabilities Act (IDEA) through parent training initiatives. You can find out more at ParentCenterHub.org/find-your-center. Many parents rely on free help, including special education attorneys or consultants, whose fees can sometimes be reimbursed once a school district approves your child's IEP.

PUBLIC VERSUS PRIVATE

As you explore the options for your neurodiverse child's education, you might feel torn between the flexibility of private schools and the training and expertise of public school teachers.

Be sure to do your research and avoid relying on preconceived notions. While some areas of the country have a large selection of evidence-based, well-funded, low teacher-to-student-ratio private school options, these choices are not available everywhere. And many public schools have amazing ratings from GreatSchools .org (a national nonprofit that rates schools based on publicly available data).

If your school does not have a strong program in place for your neurodiverse child, a few groups offer in-person or online training to schools in collaborative problem-solving and ABA principles. (ThinkKids.org has a directory of certified trainers.)

Here are some important questions to ask yourself to determine what's best for your child:

1. What are my child's top three needs, and how does the school I'm considering or communicating with meet those needs?

2. If the public school doesn't meet my needs, how much emotional energy am I willing to expend fighting them for accommodations, compared with switching to a private school where things will likely be easier?

3. Realistically, how far from home or work will I be able to drive to get my child to and from school?

4. If the school is far away, how will I adapt to my kid not having local friends for playdates?

5. Instead of a public or private school, is there a charter school that would better suit my child's needs?

6. Considering the large increase in distance learning and hybrid online models, especially beginning with the COVID-19 pandemic, is remote learning effective for my child, compared with being in a classroom?

7. If cost is a factor, does the school offer tuition assistance? Will the school district foot the bill if I can demonstrate a private school offers something the public school does not?

8. Can my child and I meet the teacher?

I consider that final question to be the biggest determinant. The teacher will really make or break your child's education experience. No matter what the school's methods or rules are, if a teacher makes your child feel alive and excited to learn, that school is the one for them.

IEP VERSUS 504

Most schools will be very agreeable to make accommodations that don't cost a lot for your child but will resist offering more extensive IEP accommodations, and most public school districts refuse to list the services they fund. You may have to be persistent to find out; if you don't know what they offer, you will miss out on potentially beneficial services for your child. If you make specific requests for accommodations that require little cost or time, you have a good chance of your public school agreeing to help. Generally, accommodations fall into either the 504 Plan category or the IEP.

A 504 Plan is a basic agreement between a parent, teacher, and principal of your local school. This plan usually includes simple accommodations, like moving seats, helping your child get a buddy to play with at lunch, placing your child in an afterschool homework club, and other options specific to your school.

Example: Changing your child's seat in the classroom to a location that works best for them, like moving them away from a distracting student, closer to the teacher so they can focus, or not at the desk with the uneven, squeaky legs that overwhelms their senses.

An IEP is more intense. This arrangement can include qualifying your child for a special education classroom, providing a classroom aide, or reimbursing you for educating your child at a private school.

Example: One of the first accommodations commonly offered in an IEP is to adapt the way educational material is presented to your child, based on their challenges. If a teacher gives a lot of anecdotes, the lesson will go over your neurodiverse child's head. So the IEP team may request the teacher give your child an outline of classroom material ahead of time. Teachers often resist doing so because it adds to their already overloaded plate, but frontloading the lessons in this way really helps aspie kids prepare for what they'll learn. I've seen kids view YouTube videos of the topics ahead of time and have a great conversation in class about what they watched.

Guiding Theme: The Optimum Classroom Behavior

Remember that educators appreciate the apprehension you feel when sending your child off to school. Your child means the world to you. Teachers are asking you to trust them to educate your child, protect them, and keep their interests and needs in mind, even when those needs are distinctly different than those of neurotypical kids. Using the strategies in the following sections will help your child succeed in school while learning to trust they can flourish in a classroom environment. Excellent resources for your child's teacher include *Lost at School* by Ross W. Greene, a necessary read for anyone who educates a child with Asperger's, and *The Hidden Curriculum* by Brenda Smith Myles, Melissa L. Trautman, and Ronda L. Schelvan, which explains how to teach a student with Asperger's ways to navigate school. The *Zones of Regulation* board game (ZonesofRegulation.com) also helps teach self-regulation for children with autism and Asperger's and should be available in every classroom.

UPDATES FROM TEACHERS

Wouldn't it be great to have a window into your child's classroom? The next best thing may be a teacher's summary. When you're aware of your child's successes and struggles, you can help them grow, especially when your child finds communicating with you difficult. (And let's face it, even neurotypical kids aren't likely to offer more than "fine" if you ask them how school is going.) When making this request, I suggest asking for just one or two goals to be reported at a time to keep the workload reasonable. Push for a daily report if your child is in elementary school; you can settle for a weekly report when they're in middle or high school. Request meetings when something seems problematic, but remember the goal is not to get your child in trouble but to help them solve a problem as early as possible.

Elementary School

Elementary school is the most important stage in establishing your aspie child's educational and social life. Middle school is when your child will get into a routine of how they're going to learn, how they're going to play, and how they're going to succeed. Teachers form an impression about how your child behaves and learns and will likely share this information with your child's next teacher, which may lead to your child gaining a reputation they don't deserve.

For this reason, get involved in your child's school. You want the educators and administrators to understand your child comprehensively, not just based on single events. I encourage you to share the following skills with your child, encourage them to go beyond their comfort zone, and let them know they always have your support, even when they're at school. I also urge you to form a great working relationship with your child's teacher, build friendships with the other parents, and, along the way, allow your child room to figure out a few things on their own.

LINING UP

Virtually all elementary kids struggle with lining up to transition from one activity to another during the school day. Kids with Asperger's find this activity especially challenging because though they really want to follow the rules and line up properly, they may also feel overwhelmed by the commotion of the other kids. One of the hardest things to teach a first grader with Asperger's is that the teacher is the one to correct the other children who aren't following the rules, not them. The more an aspie kid tries to enforce the teacher's rules, the more they'll be rejected by their peers.

Once kids fall into the routine, lining up becomes a lot easier. Here are two ways to help your child focus getting in a line:

Channel their imagination. "This is just like in preschool, when you held on to the rope and everyone walked together. This time, I would like for you to imagine you're holding on to an invisible rope. Pretend if you take one step to the left or right, you'll step into hot lava!"

Make getting in line familiar. "Can we practice walking in a line?" When you are out and about as a family, have everyone practice walking in a single-file line instead of next to each other.

CLASSROOM TRANSITIONS

Over the years, I've worked with quite a few kids who really struggled with the formalities of classroom transitions (that is, any time your child has to leave their seat to go somewhere else, even within the room, or must stop an activity to do anything else). Some get quite angry about this change. They already struggle trying to understand all the rules of the classroom; on top of everything else, leaving an activity they really enjoy and moving on to the next one is very frustrating. If this is true for your child, remind them frequently that leaving an activity doesn't mean you never get to come back. Compare the experience to an episode of a TV show: The episode might be over, but there will be a new one and you'll be back at a familiar place. Also acknowledge that it's okay to be upset when the time comes to stop doing something you like.

A few classroom activities in particular can be especially challenging:

Circle time can be difficult for Asperger's kids, who are often very bored with sitting around and talking. My best recommendation is to prep your child ahead of time by explaining how much they can wiggle inside their brain, if they need to, while their body keeps still. Your child might benefit from an accommodation, like the use of a fidget device or permission to stand during circle time. The aspie child's body needs to regulate itself in a way that "crisscross applesauce" doesn't address.

Classroom learning stations really help a child with Asperger's remember what they're supposed to do at each point of the day. But some might benefit from the teacher using a timer to remind them the activity isn't going to last forever. This helps them stick with an activity they don't like and helps improve their time awareness in general.

Hand washing may be the most difficult transition. Kids with Asperger's often have a sensory avoidance to washing their hands; they resist, argue, and don't use soap. The best motivator I have seen, though not a sure thing, is for the teacher to keep a stuffed animal near the sink who's proud of kids for washing their hands. Beyond this strategy, explaining how soap works and trying to get the child to be fascinated by the squeakiness of clean hands will sometimes work. If you know of any specific sensory issues, such as your child's aversion to certain kinds of soap or towels, keep the teacher in the loop.

GROUP LEARNING

If you play imagination games with your child on the spectrum, you may have encountered their insistence that anyone invited to the game must follow all of their rules. If you have an opinion, you are frustrating them and ruining the game. That tendency can be a problem in the classrooms that embrace project-based learning

(PBL), an educational model that emphasizes teamwork over intellectual ability. Most kids with Asperger's are very strong-willed, passionate leaders. As teammates, they often feel marginalized or offended if their idea isn't included in the final product.

Here are some discussion points to help your child be a harmonious team member:

> **Sharing ideas isn't a negative.** Help your child appreciate others' input by teaching them they shouldn't take suggestions from others to be a rejection. Just because the group uses another person's ideas doesn't mean that yours are terrible.

> **There's more than one way.** I often encourage kids on the spectrum to choose three potential solutions before proceeding on to larger tasks. This exercise prepares them to understand there are many suitable solutions to most problems. For example, I might ask a child to come up with three ways to get somebody's attention. They might write down:

1. Yell at them to pay attention.

2. Tap their shoulder pleasantly.

3. Look at them with piercing eyes.

All these solutions could work. To help this exercise really hit home, you might tell them to try out one solution for a problem each week and then come back to the drawing board to determine which is the most effective. Over time, your child becomes better at considering multiple solutions and choosing the one that works best for everyone, even if the idea is somebody else's.

ON THE PLAYGROUND

After I drop my kids off at school, I often watch them play on the playground with the other kids until the bell rings. Seeing how children self-organize without an adult around is fascinating. And seeing the isolated child who seems to want to join the others but apparently can't work up the nerve to speak up and go beyond their comfort zone really makes me sad.

Some kids on the spectrum are perfectly content not to get involved with other children. But for the child who would like to interact with others and needs help, give these guidelines:

Just join in the game. Don't make joining formal; don't tell them your name when you first start. Jump in, and if you make the game fun, you're included from there on out.

Start off with a compliment. If you walk up to a group of kids playing together, tell one they're really good at the game and ask them how they got so good. As they tell you, join in and say, "I'm on your team." The kid will like you and be less likely to exclude you.

Don't take the situation too seriously. Try to do well, but kids hate "try-hards" or "sweats." If you're too much of a rule enforcer, you get excluded. And of course, if you cheat, you get banned. And when you rage-quit a game, you lose respect, online or in the real world.

LUNCHTIME

I often ask schools why they tell kids that the sooner they're done with lunch, the more time they'll have to play. This practice usually leads to rushed eating or skipping the meal altogether, which is not good for anybody but especially not for kids on the spectrum, who definitely need to eat slowly and calmly. And they also need a lot of time to warm up and play. Thirty minutes to do both lunch and play isn't much time for elementary school kids. The time crunch is especially difficult for kids with Asperger's. They want to do both—eating and playing—perfectly, and will often fail because of others slowing them down or starting to play without them.

My strategy used to be to talk to the teacher and principal and ask them to make sure the other kids included the child with Asperger's. But this resulted in other kids making fun of the neurodiverse child, calling them out for being a "snitch." Instead, I recommend parents give their child plenty of snacks during snack time and a small lunch. Their child will be one of the first kids done with lunch, and their full stomach will help them self-regulate for the rest of the day.

Clubs may be a good option for lunchtime fun, but please know that encouraging your child to join clubs may not yield the end result you desire. If they join a club, they will have more acceptance by that group, but they may end up being kicked out of the group, which can be very deflating. Check with teachers and administrators for clubs that would be a good fit for your child.

DISMISSAL

A key, but often misunderstood, transition time for kids with Asperger's is when they're sitting in a parent's car after school without a teacher or another student observing them. So many parents tell me about the terror they feel, knowing their kid is going to kick the seat, yell and scream at them, and throw things as they drive away from the school.

Teachers often tell me they don't really believe a parent who tells them their child had such a huge meltdown so quickly after leaving the school. So I ask them: How would you feel if you had to pretend to be someone else for seven hours and then were allowed to be yourself? The teacher typically tells me they would relax. I would, too. But kids on the spectrum have difficulty expressing their pent-up anger and frustration, so their feelings come out in unhealthy ways. Neurodiverse kids usually tell me they go off on their parents because they know their parents are the only people who would never leave them. I then remind them that the people who will never leave them are usually the people they should treat best.

If this problem is intractable for your child, a therapist can help. In my practice, I teach kids how to cry, how to complain, how to vent, and how to love the person who's there to listen to them.

Otherwise, here is the best solution I have come up with: Have a snack and a preferred activity ready for them when they get in the car. If they are distracted by soothing activities, the need to explode may decrease. If they start yelling or kicking, pull over and let them get their feelings out. Don't judge or remind them about the rules you have about yelling and kicking the seat. Ask them questions about their frustration—the discussion may uncover an issue that needs to be resolved, like bullying. But even if there's not a specific reason, when your child feels understood, they won't break the rules as much and will likely apologize.

Middle School and High School

Now, on to the hardest two years of any child's life, especially those with Asperger's. Seventh graders form cliques and alliances that rarely include a child on the spectrum. Children of this age group then point out each other's flaws excessively, and randomly, throughout the day. They'll notice what you're most insecure about and remind you, or just make you insecure in other ways.

Girls on the spectrum often prefer to do their own thing during this time, rather than try to follow the crowd, which can be very lonely. Boys on the spectrum often get mad and argue or fight with other kids who keep picking on them.

In high school, neurodiverse kids have a bit of an advantage academically, but are typically at least a year or two behind their peers socially. Some kids with Asperger's adapt to this environment well and form their own cliques based on their own interests. Other kids get more isolated and go through the school day barely noticed by others. Loneliness is incredibly sad: Asperger's or not, I have yet to meet a kid who didn't have at least some interest in connecting with others. But sometimes aspie kids dissociate from their feelings about social connections as a coping mechanism.

As a parent, understanding the biological changes teenagers go through in adolescence will help both of you adapt. Teach your teenager self-advocacy, self-regulation, and a good comeback to bullying and their high school experience can be filled with the acceptance and excitement they deserve. Here are a few suggestions to help them succeed.

FOLLOWING TEACHER INSTRUCTIONS

Most parents of a child on the spectrum have become used to teachers telling them their child is very smart but struggles to follow directions. The teachers are often confused as to whether the child was actually paying attention. To address this, let your child know that teachers are easy to please if you: 1) Don't create drama for them, and 2) Don't insult them. Two rules can help:

Hold your comments until later. If you have something really useful to say related to what the teacher's talking about, wait and see if anyone else brings up what you're thinking and allow them to speak. If the point doesn't come up, email the teacher later to say you appreciated the lecture and share with them what you had been thinking in class. Teachers are usually touched when their students really care about the content of the lesson. Kids with Asperger's care.

Never correct them. Whatever you do, do not correct the teacher in front of the other students, even if you are absolutely right. Teachers are holding on to whatever respect they receive from their kids and don't appreciate being undermined. Share what happened with your family around the dinner table instead.

DEFENDING THEMSELVES

I am a pacifist in most circumstances. But in my practice, I've seen way too many kids with Asperger's contemplate suicide because they're being bullied and don't have the approval of their parents to fight back. Whenever kids feel stuck, with no way out, those with Asperger's will be significantly more likely than neurotypical kids to consider suicide to solve the problem. This is why I prefer for them to have an option to fight, rather than risk suicidal ideation.

Over the years I've gone through quite a few strategies about self-defense for kids on the spectrum. Here's my latest advice for them, in steps of increasing escalation:

1. **Defer.** If somebody is trying to start a fight with you, ask them directly if they're trying to start a fight with you. Often, they are quite surprised and will just say yes. You can then respond with, "I'm not up for fighting today, but maybe tomorrow." This unexpected response can cause them to lose interest.

2. **Defuse.** If they continue to bully you, tell them, "It looks like you were trying to make me feel bad; what you did worked. Now what?" Most of the time the bully will either be satisfied by the admission or be confused and walk away.

3. **Disengage.** If they actually hit you or otherwise get physical, turn around, run, and tell an adult you know what happened. Let your parents know and let the principal know. Bullying is not okay. Ask your parents to enroll you in self-defense classes.

4. **Defend.** If the incident is repeated, use the moves you learned in self-defense class.

AFTER SCHOOL

To see your child engaging in an afterschool activity they really love is a beautiful thing. For children on the spectrum, an afterschool program or club provides a sense of connection outside of the classroom with less intense pressure or guidance. I've seen quite a few kids thrive in an afterschool group when they're struggling elsewhere. When their passion is ignited by participating in a group activity they enjoy, a neurodiverse kid's anger usually decreases. They're more enjoyable to be around, and you'll get to celebrate their strengths.

Finding these opportunities for your child can be challenging; here's some advice to help:

Follow their passions. As always, tapping into your child's interests provides a powerful motivator. Encourage them to pursue a topic they love and they'll likely find a group dedicated to this subject.

Try these starting points. If your child's struggling to find something they're comfortable participating in, some common interests I've noticed among neurodiverse kids include band, debate club, individual sports (tennis, track, golf, or other sports where each team member competes individually), scouts, and faith-based youth groups.

Reach out. Make the most of your network and ask other parents with neurodiverse children what their kids are involved in. Be willing to get a little creative and work with the other parents to plan events for kids who need activities. For example, before the pandemic, my area had great Friday night pizza and gaming event opportunities.

Look online. Don't overlook the benefits of an online community. I've known many kids who have found a supportive, caring, and understanding tribe online by sharing a *Minecraft* server or talking about favorite anime or games via Discord. No matter which group or platform your child joins, the activity they're doing is preferable to after school loneliness. Just be sure they follow age-appropriate online safety guidelines.

Don't force the point. Encouraging a child with Asperger's to push past their comfort zone can be good for them. I've heard some great stories of kids who had a fun time after initially resisting an activity. Just be wary of trying to force a child with Asperger's to do something. Doing so rarely ends well; even neurotypical kids can resent you for making them do an activity they don't like.

If your child avoids any form of afterschool activity, even relating to subjects they're passionate about, explore the emotional reasons that may be at the root of their reluctance. Fear they'll be rejected, mocked, or ridiculed is often a concern for neurodiverse kids. Cognitive behavioral therapy and collaborative problem-solving (see pages 31 and 36) can help.

ONLINE SCHOOL

With the onset of the COVID pandemic, more kids are engaged in online school, at least part of the time, than ever before, which means the playing field is somewhat leveled for kids with Asperger's. They have a higher chance of succeeding socially when face-to-face communication isn't as important. Connecting in an online forum can depend on making a good joke, and kids with Asperger's are funny. (There's even a documentary about "Asperger's Are Us," a comedy troupe formed by four kids with Asperger's.) I know many kids on the spectrum who are meme masters; they're up on all the best and latest memes and create their own to share.

One downside of online learning is that procrastination kicks in for neurodiverse kids a bit more than for the neurotypical child. Emotion-based planning can help them get projects done sooner rather than later. To use emotion-based planning, you attach to the emotion you want to feel to motivate you to complete a task. If your child says "I want to feel proud of myself by getting a portion of my large project done today," they have a much higher chance of making progress.

With online schooling, kids who have Asperger's can learn more effectively and maintain their comfort zone at the same time. As long as they learn and do occasionally connect with other kids without developing a gaming addiction, we have succeeded. Overall, the online format allows aspie kids to thrive. Let's encourage this practice!

6

Strategies When Out and About

When helping your child self-regulate outside your home, remember there is no need to be embarrassed by a medical condition. When you prioritize your child's ability to tolerate stress and discomfort, they are more confident and hopeful. In this chapter, I will share some tips that may turn a trip to the grocery store into a bonding adventure.

The Fundamentals

Remember, there is no behavior to be embarrassed about when your child is on the spectrum. They have a medical condition that causes them to act differently. That other people misunderstand, judge, or stare rudely is not your fault. **Your main goal is to help your child successfully expand their comfort zone,** which, in turn, makes their world less overwhelming, scary, and intimidating. Everything else is just details! There are difficult moments along the way, sure. But when you prioritize your child's ability to tolerate distress, and see them confidently navigate an unpredictable situation that used to give them trouble, you will be filled with a sense of pride and hope.

Kids on the spectrum seek routine and predictable environments they can control. As you'll recall, they rely heavily on deductive reasoning, so figuring out what's likely to occur in an unfamiliar situation is difficult for them. Because they don't have the facts they crave, they may overthink all the possible outcomes of a social interaction. When you never know what someone's going to say or do next and you're trying to be ready for any possibility, feeling overwhelmed is understandable.

Neurodiverse children feel this apprehension with most people they're not familiar with and even with a few people they are comfortable with. Here are the two important strategies to keep their anxieties from being triggered when you're out and about:

Frontload, frontload, frontload. Tell them where you are going, who you are going to see, and how they can seek safety if needed. Frontloading is like giving your kid a movie trailer for how their day is going to happen. Many kids on the spectrum prepare for the next day's agenda by using *cognitive rehearsal*, a strategy of imagining what's going to happen and how they're going to handle each situation. You can help them rehearse ahead of a possibly stressful event by describing possible scenarios and adding, "which is also safe." If your child is concerned about going to a birthday party, you might tell them, "A kid you don't know may say hello to you. You can say hello back. You can tell them your name, which is also safe. You can ask them what school they go to, which is also safe." And so on. The more you can emphasize that any outcome is likely a safe outcome, the more you'll decrease their avoidance.

Carry some comfort. When in an unfamiliar setting, reassure your child that even though the situation is new, the people they're with are the same and your ability to keep your child safe is the same. Tell them about as many familiar things in that setting that you can. Keep them prepped with a backpack of favorite items that can help them self-soothe. And keep in mind that even when things are going well, your child can take a break and get their emotions back to baseline. I often use the saying, "Go slower to go faster." Pace yourself and adapt to your child's needs and your trip or outing will be more successful than trying to rush through things and provoking a meltdown.

Guiding Theme: Special Social Events

Some of the most challenging, frustrating, or embarrassing events for parents of children on the spectrum occur at major social occasions, such as a wedding, funeral, or sibling's school event. Helping our neurodiverse children stay calm while tolerating our own fear or discomfort about their difficulties coming out in front of strangers may seem like a tall order. But remember you and your family do deserve to have a great time when you're at a party or celebration, and prioritizing and preparing for the events that matter most to you is okay. Let's take a look at some particularly challenging scenarios and the solutions to help you and your neurodiverse child enjoy them.

ATTENDING BIRTHDAY PARTIES

Parents of children with Asperger's may find a noticeable lack of birthday party invites for their child. So, when they do receive one, naturally you want to make the most of the situation. And if your child does connect with someone at the party, they have a great opportunity to expand their friendship group. Here are two helpful ways to make this a successful outing:

Scope out the territory. If a party is at a park, an arcade, or some other public or commercial venue your child's never been to, take them there ahead of time to make the place familiar. Map out potential triggers and let them have some fun while you're there. This familiarity decreases the odds your child will get into conflict with other kids for their turn at a game, become upset over the food, or melt down when it's time to leave.

Practice some parent speak. Have your child rehearse a few complimentary lines to say to the birthday child's parents. The two big compliments I recommend are "You really put a lot of effort into this party" and "This is the party of the year." Often, the parent will come to you with a reaction like "Wow, your child was really nice; we should have you over sometime." I've seen this lead to a lot more playdates than successfully playing with the birthday child.

PARTICIPATING IN SPORTS

Sports help kids exercise and get strong, as well as teach competition and how to be graceful in winning and losing. Many parents hope that their child will find a sport they love, one that builds their self-esteem and in which they will successfully compete. Challenger League is a great resource for kids with a significant disability. If your child is high functioning, I encourage you to sign them up for traditional leagues. Otherwise, you might organize a group of neighborhood kids to play, which is often just as much fun, as you guide your child through the unstructured game.

In my experience, most neurodiverse kids are overwhelmed by contact sports or dislike ball sports. But sports are not necessarily out of reach for them. Try this approach:

Ask open-ended questions. If your child strongly resists the idea of team sports, think of sports as a continuum. Ask them open-ended questions about activities they would enjoy, and express your support for them to do the things they like. Then develop a list until you land on something that overlaps with their interests. Think beyond the familiar games of baseball, basketball, and football. There are plenty of other options that may be the right fit for your child, from golf to tennis to swimming to archery.

Example:

Parent: What do you like to do when you go outside?

Child: I don't know. Come back inside?

Parent: Seriously. I was thinking about sports and what you may enjoy, and I wanted to figure out what you like so we can figure out something you won't think is too boring or stressful.

Child: I don't want to play sports. I may get hurt, other kids cheat, and I suck at throwing a ball.

Parent: Those are all good points. Did you know there are sports that don't have any of those problems?

Child: No, there aren't.

Parent: What do you think the possibility is that there are other sports out there we haven't explored?

Child: You're still talking about this, aren't you? I tuned you out like a minute ago.

Parent: OK, I looked up sports for kids with Asperger's. Can I tell you about what I found for less than two minutes?

Child: Sure.

Parent: The best sports we haven't thought of are archery, climbing, parkour, tennis, golf, bowling, cross country, surfing, skateboarding, and band.

Child: Band isn't a sport.

Parent: Have you ever tried to walk in a coordinated pattern with 100 other people while playing an instrument in a heavy outfit? Doing so makes you sweat. Band counts.

Child: Are we done yet?

Parent: Sure, but can we look up some of these sports sometime?

Child: I guess.

Later

Parent: Are you up for talking about sports?

Child: Sure. I actually looked up some of the sports. I would try archery because shooting an arrow sounds fun. I didn't realize archery was a sport, and I don't have to interact with anybody. I also would try climbing because I saw that movie about the kid who climbed the mountain in Yosemite. I would be interested in figuring out how to climb big things.

Don't coach them. When they are on a team, let your child play in a way in which they feel comfortable. Allow them to explore the sport and the social aspects at their own pace rather than yours. Leave correcting your child's form and building their skills to the team coach. Watching your child be really proud of their performance is such a great feeling. If you give them excessive feedback, they may develop a strong inner critic who doesn't allow them to be happy.

BORING STUFF

Having to sit through a boring event no matter who's with us or where is a key challenge of childhood. (Even adults can have trouble doing so.) It's especially true for the neurodiverse child. To them, getting up and doing something else is just so simple, so why not do what they want? Yet allowing them to do so will mean they miss out on the social reasons to tolerate the distress.

Most kids on the spectrum are not aware of the body's reactions when they have anxiety. At events where they're bored and feeling stressed, they may not realize they are about to explode until they've already done so. For these situations, teaching them self-regulation techniques helps. They can practice at home and call on what they've learned when they need to sit still for a prolonged time. Here are a few to try (see more details and other examples on my website, MichaelUram.com):

Self-massage: Do a body scan and rub any part of the body that aches or feels restless.

Melting meditation: Imagine the body is made of ice. Pretend this ice is slowly melting into a puddle. Let all the muscles slowly relax as they melt into water.

Chocolate challenge: Place a piece of chocolate, like a Hershey's Kiss, on your tongue. The challenge is to keep your mouth closed and see how long you can keep the chocolate in place without letting the candy melt. A calm body, breathing in through the nose to cool down the mouth, and keeping your tongue still (no talking) will help. The longer kids can focus on the chocolate in their mouth, the longer they can sit for an extended period.

WEDDINGS

Pulling off a successful wedding attendance means arranging a routine-friendly, sensory-friendly, and meltdown-free time. Here are strategies I've seen work:

If possible, visit the venue ahead of time to give your child some familiarity with the setting. Frontload by talking through any concerns they have.

If your child is really invested in seeing the ceremony, prep them to be satisfied during the vows: Have a bit of non-crunchy food available, a toy they would enjoy peacefully holding, a music player with headphones, or whatever will help them keep calm and self-soothe.

Kids on the spectrum often have poor coordination and dance very awkwardly. Extended family members may try to force your child to dance with them, which often induces a panic attack. During dance time, remind your child you'll protect them from random relatives coming over and asking them to dance. If they want to get up and dance, tell them you'll go with them and will do your best to allow them to move their way.

Be prepared for a meltdown. Have an exit strategy, whether sitting on the aisle near a door or going for a walk when the reception hall gets crowded. Watch for signs of restlessness so you can move them to a quiet place sooner rather than later. Consider having a backup caretaker on duty who can help if absolutely necessary. Some families have their child's ABA specialist attend a wedding with them.

FUNERALS

You cannot reschedule your grieving. If your child struggles with being flexible at funerals, try the following:

Arrive early, pay your respects when there isn't a large crowd, and sit at the end of an aisle so you can ease out of the services if need be.

Encourage your child to study the process, if they are not engaged in mourning the loss of the loved one. Tell them they can ask you questions afterward.

Participate in only a portion of a funeral if necessary to avoid your child's meltdown during the service.

Consider carrying and handing out TACA "My Child Has Autism" cards (available at TACAnow.com) to judgmental bystanders. The cards explain the symptoms of autism. Even if you don't use them, having them available can ease your concern about explaining a difficult situation to strangers.

Bring a trusted friend, relative, or care professional to help with your child's emotional regulation so you can properly engage with the service. And while for most events I put the onus on the general public to be more flexible, in this case it's more important to protect the grieving family from distractions. Consider whether it would be better for your child not to attend.

Guiding Theme: Other Interactions and Experiences

Our daily routines can sometimes have unexpected challenges for children with Asperger's. We may have to wait a long time for our food in a restaurant. We may get to a store to buy their favorite toy, only to find the item is sold out. We may be on a vacation when a thunderstorm ruins our plans for a day at the beach. Let's talk about how to make these occasions successful, rather than dreaded.

IN STORES

Many parents tell me about the struggles they have shopping for groceries with their neurodiverse child. Here are my recommendations to enable both of you to really enjoy your trip to the grocery store:

Have a clear list. Assign favorite foods for your child to find.

Follow the same path. Create a systematic, aisle-by-aisle pattern through the entire store to follow each time so they don't run ahead or argue about where to go next.

Limit your time. Don't spend more than an hour shopping. If you need to take more time, plan for two trips.

Stay on task. If there are hiccups in finding something on the list, drop the task and save the item for the next trip. Interruptions and tangents overwhelm kids on the spectrum.

When you're at a clothing store:

Educate your child as much as possible about the clothes they already have and why you need to go shopping for them or yourself. Talk about how the fit of clothing affects their comfort. Essentially, the more your child buys into the need to go shopping and develops positive emotions about the experience, the more tolerant they will be. If they have a decent explanation about the trip ahead of time, they don't get frustrated with you for shopping.

Use emotion-based planning. Talk to them about the emotions you feel when you wear a new outfit. Use your response to suggest how they may feel when they try new clothing. When you focus on managing their emotions, rather than convincing them of societal norms, you have a higher chance of success.

AT RESTAURANTS

If you've been avoiding restaurants because of your child's behavior, here are a few tips to make the trip worth the effort:

Prioritize. Start by working on the difficulties that frustrate you most. Doing so will make it easier to have some successful restaurant experiences, even if there's room for improvement.

If your child's a picky eater, explore the boundaries of their preferences at home first so they become used to the type of food available at the restaurants you'd like to visit.

Accommodate your child's sensory issues by permitting them to use headphones, an iPad or device, or other objects for self-soothing. Making use of these things is not embarrassing if your child honestly struggles to maintain their attention while waiting for their dinner to be served. Do attempt to have a small conversation with them; you may get to connect, even if briefly. But expecting them not to have a device or fidget may be unreasonable.

VACATIONS

Many parents just like you dream of a vacation, only to feel guilty for dreaming of having a vacation without the usual parenting dilemmas they face. This is normal! And while few vacations live up to our dreams, if you try these three practices, you'll stand a good chance of making happy, connected vacation memories:

Involve them. Get your child's input into where they'd like to go. Have them help with researching and planning to whatever degree they're able. If you engage them for at least a portion of the trip, there's a greater likelihood they'll tolerate parts they don't like.

Make lots of stops. Take more frequent breaks or stops than you usually would to help them self-regulate. Don't wait until they seem to need the change: A neurodiverse kid often won't tell you they need to self-soothe or stretch their legs. But they almost certainly will do something that frustrates others when they start to hit their limit.

Get them ready. Frontload your child by discussing ways the trip will be enjoyable for them, and remind them they can take a 15-minute quiet break at any time.

Pace yourselves. Don't set yourself and your child up to be rushed and irritated. It is okay to slow down your routine so everyone manages the ups and downs.

AT THE THEME PARK

Plan ahead for the emotions you would like your child to experience at a theme park. If you want them to feel wonder and excitement, you don't need to go on every ride in the park. A slower-paced, emotional goal–based visit gives you and your family a greater chance of a fun, successful day.

Waiting in line is a struggle for all kids, so many theme parks will make exceptions to decrease the stress for children with special needs. When planning your trip, investigate options for front-of-the-line passes and other accommodations.

Remember what your child's attention span limit is and plan activities to do while waiting in line. With so many unknowns, frontloading is especially important at a theme park. Bring your child's favorite snacks, drinks, and games to make waiting in any line less boring and more engaging. Also, be aware of their sensory issues when choosing rides. Do not pressure them onto a ride they don't want to try, even if you think they'll enjoy the experience once they get on. Even if they eventually like the ride, they will remember you trying to control the experience and possibly not want to come back.

CLOTHES

Many teenagers with Asperger's tell me they're often uncomfortable with the feeling of most clothing. And they're usually not looking to impress others with style of fashion; some even tell me they wear clothes only so other people don't look at them.

Clothes come with many sensory triggers that make wearing them an unpleasurable experience for kids with Asperger's. Here are three tips to consider when figuring out your child's relationship with clothing. I also suggest consulting with an occupational therapist who specializes in Asperger's to help decrease the intensity of their sensory distress.

Favor tagless shirts and seamless socks and underwear to minimize irritation. The Taylor Bug Kisses foundation (TaylorBugKisses .com) has a list of retailers that sell sensory-friendly clothes.

Trust your child when they tell you they do not like certain clothes but can't explain why. They're probably not making up a reason to complain; many neurodiverse kids aren't sure why something is uncomfortable for them.

Tolerate them wearing the same thing over and over again if they always want to wear a favorite shirt or outfit and doing so improves their mood. Wash frequently or buy several of the same item, possibly in different colors.

7

Strategies for in the Moment

At this point in the book, you're now equipped with several chapters' worth of advice on how to handle all sorts of situations. Notice how a common theme has been the importance of planning ahead, frontloading, and being proactive. Preparing for *every* eventuality, however, is impossible. Life does not work in this way, especially with Asperger's in the picture. So in this chapter, we'll have lots of advice for what you can do in the moment, when problems arise and you don't have time to plan. We're going to walk through a hypothetical day in your child's life, examining the challenges from their point of view. And at each step, we'll discuss a few tools you can use to make things easier.

A Day in the Life of . . .

As we move through one day in your child's life, we're going to discuss specific goals and emotions I would like you both to feel. Before we get started, here are a few general notes to keep in mind regarding time of day:

The morning is generally not a great time to create conflict if either of you hasn't had a good night's rest. I would let go of some expectations on days when you or your child is dealing with a lack of sleep. Noticing a good time to encourage your child to be flexible—or not—gives you have a better chance of improving their morning routine.

The afternoon is best for encouraging your child to grow. Whether educational time, working with a therapist, or cleaning up their room, I've noticed the middle of the day seems to be the ideal time for your child to shine. For younger children, I suggest scheduling most playdates between 10 a.m. and 4 p.m.

In the evening, the best strategy to connect with your teenage child is to help them develop boundaries for homework time, social time, family time, and dinner. If these things are set in stone, the routine may annoy them but the predictability makes conflicts less likely to arise. A family that doesn't follow set routines often experiences more disagreements, disappointments, and frustrations.

In the Morning

In my practice, I've spent lots of time developing recommendations for parents who want their child to have a successful day at school by getting up on time and getting out the door with very little stress. For kids with Asperger's, it can be quite a challenge to accomplish this feat. I've found knowing what *doesn't* work is a big help.

Rushing them never works. When you're patient with your child, you give them the chance to self-regulate and achieve a goal. When you rush them, they get overwhelmed and often lose their temper, sabotaging any effort to speed things up.

Consequences never work in the long term. Appreciation and encouraging words enable kids to feel proud of themselves and ready to expand their comfort zone. Rewards are only temporary motivators, and negative consequences lead them to fear your judgment.

Yelling does not work. Calm words lead them to hear you more clearly, which increases their chances of complying with your request. When you yell, they stop hearing you and become fearful.

Keep those points in mind as we look at best practices for starting the day.

WAKING UP

Kids on the spectrum often need more sleep than neurotypical kids. Unfortunately, the vast majority struggle to get a good night's sleep. It's very important to teach them to notice whether they've slept well. With this awareness, they are more likely to be on board with strategies to wake up in a good mood.

For kids who often wake up in the middle of the night, I suggest keeping a self-soothing item next to their bed. Try a good book, a toy, a fidget device—anything that works and will help them relax. Here are a few more bedside recommendations:

Get an alarm they like. A loud, annoying wake-up sound will likely anger them, which sabotages your goal from the start, so let them choose one. If your child tends to break things, look for an alarm that's cheap and easily replaceable.

For older kids, I recommend using a voice-controlled, highly customizable, and easy-to-set alarm, like a digital device or an AI virtual assistant.

If your child has no problem getting up in the morning, but in fact gets up too early, discuss with them an appropriate time they can come out of their room.

For little ones who are too-early risers, have a quiet toy box in their room they can play with until their alarm goes off. Or set up a quiet time corner with books and drawing supplies. If you don't want to use an alarm clock, tape up a piece of paper showing the desired wake-up time. When their clock matches the time on the paper, they're allowed to wake you up.

EATING BREAKFAST

Generally, the adage that eating a good breakfast is important before starting your day is true for kids with Asperger's. The only exception is if your child is taking stimulant medication, in which case it can be difficult for them to eat right away.

Here are four ways to make breakfast time easier—two proactive options for when you can plan ahead and two in-the-moment reactive solutions:

Proactive: A prepared, probably cooked meal in line with your child's dietary needs will likely require at least 10 minutes of prep time. Use this routine when the morning is going well.

Reactive: When the schedule is off the rails, give your child a banana or apple and milk to eat quickly either while you're driving to school or in less than five minutes at the table.

Proactive: Let your child choose the morning meal they'd like on good days. Have them try out a few different meals so you'll have options within their comfort zone.

Reactive: If a rushed morning cuts breakfast short, your child packs extra snacks in their backpack in line with what they will actually eat, rather than what's healthiest. Kids usually choose dry cereal, Goldfish, or a snack bar.

GETTING DRESSED

I can't tell you how many stories I've heard about children arguing over what they're going to wear, taking up 10 to 15 minutes each morning, with frustrated parents adding if their child would just choose their clothes 10 minutes sooner, they wouldn't be having an issue over and over again.

Sound familiar? Try these solutions:

Preparation: Have your child choose four or five different outfits they like, and store the combinations (pants plus socks plus top, etc.) together. This makes choosing in the morning so much easier.

Meditation: Have them meditate with you, or alone, for five minutes every morning before getting dressed. I've seen so many kids have a much better day when they slow down their brain to go faster.

Learning to slow down their body through meditation is incredibly helpful for kids with Asperger's. There are many great websites, videos, and books for kids on the spectrum to follow. A good starting point is looking at the meditation and mindfulness options for autism available at AutismKey.com.

Before School

If you're a parent who dreads the morning routine, you're not alone. Many parents of neurodiverse kids tell me of the struggle they have motivating their child to do basic hygiene and everything else needed to get ready for school in the morning. I've had parents feel relieved when I remind them they don't have to take responsibility for their middle school and high school child being late to class. Self-regulating is your child's responsibility. Parents are responsible to do their best to guide their child, but not control them. Let's look at some ways to provide good guidance.

GETTING READY FOR SCHOOL

When you look into your child's backpack, do you see a random mess of papers, old snacks, and icky surprises? These steps are for you:

1. In the moment, when you discover this chaos, ask your child without sarcasm what they see. Hear them out, and then ask if they would like your opinion.

2. If they agree to talk about the situation, ask them if after school—not now—you can go through their backpack with them and maybe help them become less overwhelmed with organizing their bag.

3. Revisit the subject at a time when you're both calm. Have them take the lead in organizing their things; let them develop a strategy on their own, and have them try out their strategy for a week. If you give too much of your opinion, they'll feel ashamed and will be rude to you.

4. If their plan helps, give them praise. If what they've done needs improvement, first ask them if they would like to continue on this path, given that the first step was a good start.

5. If they say yes but they don't know what else to do, offer one suggestion to try out for the week.

6. Keep at your attempts for organization. Slow but steady progress leads to long-term change.

LEAVING ON TIME

We need to get to school on time without question. You have a time crunch and need to move on to your daily responsibilities. Your kids need to be in a good, calm state of mind when school starts. But there will be days when these goals don't coexist very well. And the more you rush a child with Asperger's, the more likely they'll have an overwhelmed meltdown that takes even more time to resolve. Here's how to handle a rough morning:

Going slower to go faster is key at this time. Find a few minutes to meditate or otherwise calm yourself down so you can proceed more effectively. Have your child use any self-soothing practices they know.

Prioritize getting yourself ready first, then your child. The last thing you want to feel is anger and resentment toward your child because you don't have enough time to get ready yourself.

Consider using a virtual home assistant to give everyone a reminder of each step of their morning routine. Your child won't argue with a voice assistant like they will with a parent. Charts or other visual references taped to the wall or a song about the sequence of steps of getting ready can also work well.

Use behavioral chaining, meaning repeatedly doing a series of activities in the same order over and over to increase your chances of remembering. Practice the steps with your child and have them follow the same steps every day. The events before and after help you remember each step.

Build a buffer. When you work out the morning schedule, include extra time—20 minutes, if possible—to account for unexpected delays.

Accept that this morning isn't going the best, and trust there's hope for more peaceful mornings to come.

GETTING TO SCHOOL

The sensory issues neurodiverse kids deal with often come into play when they're riding in vehicles, especially unfamiliar ones. Here are a few recommendations that take into account a child's unstated needs:

Walking to school, if this is an option, is a great way for kids to feel regulated, get their wiggles out, and have a greater chance of focusing on school.

Riding a bike is great exercise, but many kids with Asperger's have difficulty with coordination that can make this dangerous with distracted morning commuters on the road. If possible, ride to school with them on your own bike.

The school bus is a safe option physically, but for neurodiverse kids is often a more dangerous option socially. With no adult supervision, kids on buses talk about taboo topics more often than in any other place. Bullying behaviors are also more likely to go unnoticed. If your child does ride the bus, suggest they sit in the first few rows. Encourage them to be assertive with other kids. Most important, be sure they know if something makes them feel uncomfortable, they need to tell a trusted adult.

Driving the kids to school may not be the way you were brought up, but doing so is not as unusual as you may think. (In California, where I am, most parents drive their kids to school and this practice is more common than children riding a bus.) Besides averting some of the above issues, having some personal connection time in the car with your child can help the day get started just right for both of you.

After School

After school is the time to help your child unwind from the day, do some preferred activities, handle a few challenges, get into their comfort zone, and just generally recharge and connect. Here are some ways to smooth over the rough spots.

HANGING OUT WITH FRIENDS

For some parents of kids with Asperger's, an issue over their child hanging out with friends would be a welcome problem. Parents often tell me they can't get their kid to talk to another child, let alone call one of them a friend. If you're in this situation, here are a few strategies to set up some interactive time:

Have a light touch. Kids with Asperger's are rarely motivated to share their interests with other kids, play a two-player game, or have a typical get-to-know-you conversation with a peer. I would not try encouraging any of these activities first. They need to make social connections in their own way.

Build on their inclinations. Consider what emotionally engages your child and create opportunities for them to get necessary information about their interests from relevant peers. For example, if your child is excited about the *Avatar: The Last Airbender* cartoon being back on Netflix, they might plan an afternoon for other kids to come over and watch the show (or the sequel, *The Legend of Korra*).

Support a project. Help them develop a project they'd like to work on, something that holds interest for them. Choose something that will require them to engage other kids to accomplish specific tasks they can't do alone. Craft projects or assembly kits for model rockets, robots, solar panels, and other engineering projects are good candidates for a group activity with delegated assignments.

Keep your eyes open. Be alert for opportunities. Follow your child's lead any time they seek to connect with another kid. Also be watchful for opportunities to create new social opportunities around similar, but not identical, topics. Often, kids with Asperger's don't realize that if another child's interest is in the same category as their own, they might enjoy sharing with each other. For example, a child who's into *Magic: The Gathering* cards might have fun exploring *Yu-Gi-Oh!* cards.

Accept glitches. If your child becomes frustrated in a social setting, don't force them to interact with others. Listen to their frustrations and ask if you can help solve the problem. You may have a chance at repairing a misunderstanding or creating an opportunity for more socialization. For example, I often hear of people with Asperger's getting mad at others for lying, when in reality, the situation changed and plans were postponed.

SPORTS

As discussed in the last chapter (see page 112), getting kids involved in sports is a great idea. Forcing them to do so is a terrible idea. The guiding principle is to encourage them to get involved and to allow them to quit if they don't like the activity. Reminding them they're obligated to the coach and the team results in them resisting trying new things. And for kids with Asperger's, the last thing you want is for them to avoid expanding their comfort zone. Keep these points in mind:

Don't micromanage. If your child struggles with the social components of team sports, allow them to interact with teammates at their own pace.

Look beyond soccer. Individual team sports and activities such as tennis, golf, swimming, cross-country running, band, and color guard balance the social interaction and physical exertion needs of aspies.

Don't discourage toe walking. I have seen no evidence that toe walking (walking on the toe and ball of the foot, rather than rocking from heel to toe) needs to be discouraged. Many people with Asperger's prefer to walk this way; the reason isn't known, but there are no negative consequences. I have had several adults with Asperger's tell me how much they were shamed and mocked for walking their natural way. My recommendation is to treat unusual traits only if they result in a serious problem.

MUSIC LESSONS

Many kids with Asperger's are drawn to music; they really love the soothing sound, the step-by-step directions of sheet music, or the individual expectations and orderliness of an orchestra.

I strongly encourage parents to let their child try music lessons if they want to. The instrument choice doesn't matter—whatever they're drawn to is best. Many adolescents aspies I meet are able to appreciate music in ways I struggle with. You may even find yourself really envying your child's enhanced auditory ability.

HOMEWORK

Homework can be a struggle for any kid, all the more so when they have sensory sensitivities, difficulty working through roadblocks, and time constraints. While there's a significant debate on the educational usefulness of homework, evidence suggests that working after school does help children learn to self-regulate, motivate themselves, ignore distractions, and achieve success. Here are a few ideas to make homework time less fraught and more productive:

Be available to assist your child with homework, but don't direct them.

Have them problem-solve their ideal strategy for getting their work done, and allow them to track how successful their choice is.

When they do struggle, intervening with suggestions is okay to increase their success and decrease frustration. Some possible suggestions include going slowly through the instructions to check comprehension, having them ask peers what strategies worked for them, and tolerating the distress of letting go of some homework and telling the teacher they had a problem with doing what was asked.

Never do their work for them. Having a student not turn in homework is always okay, as is letting the teacher know about the struggles. Our children grow through owning our short-comings and mistakes, not by denying them and certainly not by having a parent complete their homework for them. I can't tell you how many children secretly confessed to me that their parents have been doing their work for them for years, and they feel ashamed and dumb as a result.

Praise successful strategies they come up with for homework, especially ones you didn't agree with in the beginning. Realizing they had a better idea than we did really builds your child's self-esteem.

HOMEWORK VERSUS TV

Many parents ask me if they should allow their children to watch television or do other distracting activities while doing their homework. When I was first starting out as a clinician, I always said "No, encourage them to do their best with the least amount of distractions possible."

But after realizing how much of a struggle this advice was for children on the spectrum, I found research that supports *distracted focus*—letting a child have one distracting activity to do while completing homework to block out all the other distractions. You might allow them to use a fidget device or have a radio on and to intervene only if you see them becoming distracted for more than a few minutes at a time.

More recently, I've found the benefits of *emotion-based planning*. When kids with Asperger's identify the emotion they want to feel as a result of completing homework, they're more able to complete the task without a distraction.

A third helpful technique is to try *permission-based parenting*. Instead of dumping mandates on your child, ask if they'd like some suggestions that would help them get through their homework. Kids really thrive when their parents ask them if they would like any feedback on how to do things differently while allowing the child to independently reason through their strategy.

Finally, I've found that many kids with ADHD need to focus for 10 minutes, then take a 3-minute break. The pattern also works well for individuals with Asperger's.

CHORES

Children with Asperger's often avoid tasks that make no sense to them. Making your bed, dusting, vacuuming, cleaning up after pets, and other maintenance tasks can seem worthless to a neurodiverse child. Many parents have tried to get around this reluctance by attaching consequences to chore avoidance. But doing so usually doesn't work and really stresses out the child. I view avoiding chores as an awareness and skill deficit, not an issue of disobedience or laziness. Here are some suggestions for motivating your child to do chores:

Validate their confusion. Agree that if you didn't see the point of something, you likely wouldn't want to do the task either.

Ask them if they would like to learn more about the chore to help them understand the purpose.

Give them specific chores with a process they may enjoy, or have them do something that makes literal sense to them. For example, most neurodiverse kids feel a sense of pride in supplying things people need; there is logic in doing so. A few good examples are replenishing toilet paper, keeping track of grocery shopping items, mowing the lawn, sharpening pencils, or putting paper in the printer.

If your child is sensitive to odors or other sensory stimuli, I would not have them be in charge of putting out the trash or cleaning toilets. But other cleaning activities, such as mopping, vacuuming, or dusting while wearing a filtered mask could work.

In the Evening

Evening is when many parents can spend the most time with their aspie child, but this is also when dysregulation and conflict commonly arise. Similar to neurotypical children, kids with Asperger's can be exhausted at the end of the day and more prone to meltdowns. To prevent your child—and you—from feeling overwhelmed,

follow the basic principles of providing structure and giving positive reinforcement.

PREPPING FOR DINNER

Many young children with Asperger's aim to please and don't mind
setting out plates and silverware for dinner. The process of preparing a meal is attractive to many individuals on the spectrum, so
consider involving your child when getting dinner ready. Perhaps
they could follow a recipe to create a dish, or get into the repetitive, satisfying tasks of cutting vegetables or setting the table.
Here are a few suggestions to see if your child might like helping
at mealtime:

If your child has never cooked, ask them if they would like to
figure out how their favorite dish is made. Then create the meal
together. If they enjoy the process, make cooking together a
regular thing.

If your child would rather eat at their computer, I would ask
them about their reasoning. This behavior usually means they
are avoiding something, are too into a video game, or are possibly depressed. Rather than demand their compliance, explore
their thoughts.

If your child shows a lot of engagement in the process, get
them more involved in making meals at home and ask if they'd
like to enroll in cooking classes. When they're older and looking for a part-time job, restaurants might be a good place to
turn since these establishments tend to hire many teens. With
experience prepping meals and cooking at home, your child
may have an advantage over the typical inexperienced teen.
Kids with Asperger's need as many strengths as possible to
overcome a neurotypical manager's understanding of their
other aspie traits.

EATING DINNER

The evening meal can be a connecting experience with your neurodiverse child if you set up a structure. Most children with Asperger's really don't like idle chitchat, so they are not likely to look forward to dinner table conversation. Instead, maybe you could have them research a topic and present the details to everyone at dinner as a way of connecting.

Most adolescents with Asperger's can make quite a mess while eating, sometimes because they have difficulties with fine motor skills or they don't care how others perceive them. I have found that finishing classes, where young people are taught the social etiquette of fine dining, can be surprisingly helpful for many boys and girls with Asperger's. With this instruction, they finally get the guidebook on social interaction, at the dinner table and in other situations, they've always wanted.

If a food sensitivity alone is the reason your child dislikes dinnertime, explore some possibilities with a registered dietitian and develop a plan to adapt or accommodate to your child's needs.

HYGIENE

Hygiene is one of the most difficult issues for parents to handle. Kids with Asperger's don't pay much attention to others' perceptions of them and have a low desire for social interactions, so they may see little reason to prioritize cleaning rituals. As we discussed in chapter 4, sensory issues may be at the root of hygiene problems (see page 82); a new showerhead, for example, could make all the difference. I've also found depression can be a contributing factor to not following good hygiene; when I work with kids with Asperger's who aren't depressed, hygiene is rarely an issue.

BEDTIME ROUTINE

Having a consistent, calming, and effective bedtime routine is so difficult to manage. But these tactics may help you and your child end the day peacefully, setting yourselves up for an easier start the next morning.

Teens with Asperger's will likely try their best to stay up very late on the weekend and will be surprised each Monday when they find it difficult to wake up. Here are two tips:

Read the latest information on sleep with them. Research shows teens need consistent sleep much more so than younger children.

Give them validation and encouragement when they are well-rested and in a good mood in the morning.

For younger children:

Validate their intense emotions rather than minimize them. If they are very angry about bedtime, let them know you see their anger rather than telling them this isn't something to be so worked up about.

Encourage them to read before bed with a favorite book under low light. Some quiet reading will engage their racing brain and give their body time to transition to sleep.

Schedule baths, which are incredibly soothing, about an hour before bedtime as part of a nighttime routine.

Ensure they have their favorite soothing object, whether a stuffed animal or weighted blanket. Neurodiverse kids need sensory attention to help them sleep.

Weekends

Weekends are a great time to have less structure, fewer expectations, and less need for emotional regulation. In other words, this time is to relax, a precious commodity for kids with Asperger's.

In this next section, I will discuss how to have the ideal weekend. A common thread with a neurodiverse child is that you may have to adjust your family's expectations for social interaction and manage your frustrations that things can't be easier. But overall, weekends can still be relaxing, engaging, and peaceful with some accommodations.

SLEEPING IN

Adjust to your child's sleep preferences. A long exhausting week usually leads most neurotypical people to want to sleep in on the weekend. Children with Asperger's often struggle with sleep; some kids sleep in on weekends or try to sleep excessively, while others are early risers. Either way, learn your child's preference and do your best to be flexible with them on the weekends. If they are able to get a few more hours of sleep, they may be in a much better place emotionally for the rest of the weekend.

Stick to a regular bedtime. I encourage both neurotypical and neurodiverse kids to stick to their bedtime routine no matter the day of the week. Breaking your schedule to stay up late can be tempting, even for kids with Asperger's who take comfort in routine, but the disruption to their sleeping habits is often not worth the benefits.

If your child does sleep later on weekends, use the time for you and your partner to connect. I've heard many couples say they spend weekends hoping their kids will sleep in because their only intimate time is in the morning before the kids get up.

DOWNTIME VERSUS SCREEN TIME

The most common question I get from parents of neurodiverse children is: How much screen time should I allow my child to have? The correct answer: Stop counting hours. Time spent online should be considered in terms of quality rather than the quantity. Behaviors and emotions are more indicative of whether screen time is healthy, rather than the amount of time that has passed.

Your top priority is making sure your child is not using a computer, phone, or device in a way that increases their stress level, such as with games that are highly competitive or frustratingly difficult. Interacting with others is a better use of screen time (*Minecraft* is probably one of the best examples). A good gauge is your child's mood when the time is done. If they're irritable with you, the game is likely overstimulating. I also suggest a strict rule of avoiding global chat in most games (that is, communication among everyone playing the game, not just friends). The exchanges are often rather toxic.

If video games are a concern, be aware that evidence definitively shows that violent video games do not create more violent kids. Evidence does show that playing video games can be stressful, but this seems to depend on the type of game being played. Increasingly, studies are showing that playing slower-paced games can actually be relaxing. What this boils down to is there's not a mathematical formula for calculating your child's ideal screen time. You'll need to understand their engagement with their device by taking a look at what they're doing.

Many kids on the spectrum enjoy socializing on Discord, sharing memes, and playing *Minecraft, Pokémon Go,* and *Fortnite*. When I see how happy they are interacting with others, I prioritize this type of happiness over expectations that socializing should be done face-to-face. For example, if your child plays *Minecraft* in creative mode and designs amazing structures with other kids their age, this activity is very similar to building with Legos with a friend. How mad would you be with your child if they played Legos with another kid for a few hours?

MEALTIME

Imagine this dream: Everyone in your family sits down for a meal, talks about their day, and gives each other encouragement and no one looks at a phone or device while eating. While I hear unicorns do this on a regular basis, humans have a chance of having perhaps one family meal per week that approaches this ideal.

Weekend meals are a good opportunity to try, with a few helpful strategies.

Plan on the emotion you would like to feel before figuring out the food you would like to eat. For example, if you want your neurodiverse child to feel proud of their ability to expand their comfort zone, make a favorite meal of theirs with a tiny side of something extremely similar with a minor tweak. If they only eat chicken nuggets, make a different brand of chicken nuggets and put one in with the usual kind.

Regularly talk as a family about how much you want to be aware of each other's lives, hopes, excitement, so you come to the table with similar expectations.

Understand what challenges your child with Asperger's faces in participating and be as flexible as possible to accommodate their illogical, but emotionally necessary, desires.

Involve everyone in all stages of meal prep and dishwashing to create a sense of connection. The more that tasks are done together, the less children on the spectrum avoid them.

Never force a child to finish their meal. Sometimes they are so overwhelmed with the sensations of food, they have to stop eating. Default to believing them when they say they're finished, rather than pushing them to eat more.

Use an approach to food that advocates for not pushing children to a meltdown in pursuit of expanding their palate. Kids have real food sensitivity limits that should not be minimized.

EVENING OUTINGS

Weekends are a favorite time for a family evening out, whether you go to a restaurant dinner, see a movie, attend a seasonal or holiday event, or even stay overnight somewhere as part of a weekend trip. If you've found yourself feeling irritated or disappointed when a special night was ruined by your neurodiverse child's behavior, don't be too hard on yourself for having that human reaction. But to avoid a repeat, you have to understand how your child's energy levels fluctuate.

Kids with Asperger's wear a metaphorical mask all day to fit in with us. Not saying or doing the first thing that comes to their mind is exhausting, as is summoning the mental energy to deal with neurotypical social skills and routines. We all have a limited amount of energy to spend each day before we hit our breaking point. Kids with Asperger's hit this point sooner than most. When planning a night out, here are a few tips for a successful evening that won't overtax your child's depleted energy level:

Be realistic. Go on evening outings less frequently than other families do.

Check in. During the outing, ask your child how they are feeling and pay attention to their answer.

Bail out. If your child is starting to feel exhausted, leave as soon as you can. This warning sign may mean they'll have a meltdown soon.

Take a break. If going home is not possible, give your child a way to lie down or sleep, without judgment. Perhaps one parent can stay with them in the car while the rest of the family watches the movie or finishes eating.

BEDTIME

Have you ever spent the night outside in a tent in the middle of the woods? So many small sounds startle you and sleeping can be hard. Kids with Asperger's usually hear so much more than a neurotypical person does, and their minds magnify the possibility that the strange noise means something bad could occur. Here are a few suggestions to make bedtime better:

Use ritual. Kids with Asperger's develop routines around bedtime that help comfort them. Understand and track your child's routine. See what rituals help them sleep better.

Be comforting. If your young child wants to sleep in your bed, remind them you can still hear them from your bedroom.

They can easily just call for you and you will be there. You can rehearse this to reassure them.

Get your rest. As a parent, don't stay up too late. Yes, this means going to bed earlier and waking up earlier, even though this time each day is your only chance to relax. The good news is you need about two hours less sleep, on average, than your child does. Make the most of this time, but don't push further. A tired parent is an easily frustrated parent.

SUNDAY NIGHT RITUAL

For you and your neurodiverse child, getting the week off to a great start begins on Sunday night. Here are a few strategies for getting the week started right:

Sit down with your child to take a look at the week to come. Review potential triggers and come up with a plan well ahead of time. If your child has a big test on Thursday, for example, make sure you don't schedule much on Wednesday night.

Take a break if your child asks for one while you're making plans. Just going through the week's agenda can be stressful for them. Agree to that break and ask them what strategy they're going to use to relax. Then schedule a return in 15 minutes.

Have a family calendar. I prefer a shared online calendar that everyone in the family can update and change. Print out the week's agenda on Sunday and pick a visible place to post the schedule for everyone to see throughout the week.

8

Looking Ahead

Endings are a time to look ahead. In these final pages, let's consider how the new perspective you've gained enables you to truly understand your child's uniqueness, enjoy their strengths, and stand with them as they face challenges. What meaning will you make of your relationship with your child?

Parenting a child with Asperger's isn't predictable and can take everything you have to give. So always know you matter and be sure to take care of yourself emotionally, physically, relationally, and spiritually. Doing so gives you the energy to have hope and do all you can to give your child as many chances to succeed as possible.

Meaningful Parenting

Let's zoom out from the day-to-day skills you've learned and ask some questions about the bigger picture.

What are your biggest priorities for your child?

Are you remembering to experience life with your child and not just manage what happens? Many parents tell me they get so focused on improving their child's skills, they forget to pause their parent role and just play and be with their kids, independent of expectations.

Reflecting on your child's life so far, what is one experience you had with them that led you to feel loved? What experience did you have that reminded you why you wanted to be a parent in the first place? What experience did you have that made you feel love toward your child in a way only a parent can understand?

Return to these questions often. The answers may change. But remember, having Asperger's doesn't mean your child isn't going to show you love. You may not recognize that love because of the unique ways they express their thoughts and feelings. You're still in your child's heart.

Home Life

We've covered many options to help your child self-regulate. As you work out the most effective methods for preempting your child's emotional blowups, hold on to the main message: A peaceful home life *is* possible. Each success you have should convince you that you have more of an influence on your child's life than you thought. Bring your successes to mind whenever difficult moments try your patience.

Be alert for your child's growing independence. Your neurodiverse child will feel empowered to start figuring things out on their own rather than relying on you to solve their problems. When you give them the option of exiting a conflict and coming back 15 minutes later, the big arguments you used to have will become less frequent. Slowing down a clash allows everyone's adrenaline levels to drop back to baseline. With less intense emotions, you have a greater chance of solving the deeper problem behind the quarrel and preventing a repeat.

As your successes build and setbacks inevitably occur, I urge you to reflect on your parenting. Keep a journal to record the templates that enable you to get along well with your child and the frustrating times when you don't get something right. You'll create a resource to refer to when you need solutions and record a journey that will convince you that you're getting pretty good at this.

School Life

When managing your child's academic life, you'll find that your priorities are slightly different than those of school administrators. Their goal is to make sure all the kids in the classroom have the best chance to succeed through the best available tools and most caring teachers. Your goal is to do your best to be sure their goals don't minimize your child's significance. The path forward to this endeavor involves partnership and collaboration whenever possible. The best IEP (individualized educational plan) meetings occur when the principal and teacher are looking to develop a plan that works best for your child and that takes the least amount of time out of their day. Such a plan can meet their needs and help your child succeed.

This book was written during the coronavirus pandemic, which created profound changes in education, some of which will surely become permanent. Six months into emergency distance learning, I'm seeing that many neurotypical kids are struggling but that many with Asperger's are thriving in a world with greatly reduced social expectations. That said, some aspies are having difficulty in the absence of the structure provided by a classroom routine. If your child continues with virtual schooling after the quarantine ends, keep in mind they still need accommodations. I recommend exploring the option of having an in-home tutor for at least one hour per week.

Social Life

Is there anything better than seeing your child expand their social circle? As you help your neurodiverse child develop their social skills, be sure to work on your own discomfort with taking your child out and about. Let go of the responsibility of sheltering your child from the consequences of their behavior. It hurts to see them struggle or be rejected in an awkward social encounter. It's definitely not pleasant to end a restaurant visit or shopping trip because of a meltdown. But reviewing the experience with them later, when they're calm, provides a chance for them to learn from what happened.

Making friends is hard work for a child with Asperger's. But the result is a small, but solid, group of friends who respect one another, who exercise patience when things become frustrating, and who are always there on the weekend to get together. Your child might never be excited to go to the prom or even attend many birthday parties. But they can still have friends who make them happy. This happiness matters more to most parents than their child fitting the neurotypical social mold.

Make Time for Yourself

Addressing the effects of Asperger's on your family is important. But you may be surprised to hear that your own self-care is more important. Taking care of yourself is what enables you to take care of your family.

Even when you are at home with your child, establish healthy self-care exercises such as yoga, a relaxing bath, or reading time. Doing so is possible. Monitoring a neurodiverse child does take more time than monitoring a neurotypical child, but by studying the neurodiverse child's patterns, you can find pockets of time when you can let your guard down and engage in some self-soothing: a cup of tea, a phone call with a friend, some downtime on the couch with a magazine.

Taking time for yourself and having activities you do on your own is okay. A date night with your partner is healthy and will help the two of you nurture each other during a stressful week. Sharing a moment of peace and connection is what holds your relationship together when you are frustrated and exhausted.

Remind your other children how much you appreciate them and make sure you, as parents, prioritize taking them to the activities they love. Nurture the relationship between your neurotypical and neurodiverse children, but let them have their separate lives and interests, too. One parent going to one child's game or event while the other stays home with their aspie sibling is okay.

What's Wonderful about Asperger's

As challenging as life on the spectrum can be, there are many things to appreciate about your child having Asperger's. I love hearing a child with Asperger's fight for what's right, when others are cynical. I am proud of the way they're determined to do their best no matter the obstacle. I'm thoroughly impressed with their in-depth knowledge about a single topic. I completely respect the amount of concern and compassion so many kids with Asperger's have for animals. I think kids with Asperger's can make great politicians, especially when they prioritize logical, unselfish solutions. The desire for honesty I see in these kids is inspiring. The mischief they do get up to is usually rather funny and rarely mean-spirited. Their respect for the elderly outshines most other children's. Most kids with Asperger's I have met have a musical gift or a relentlessly intense expertise in a fascinating subject. I would trust a kid with Asperger's to be loyal to their friends under any circumstances. I love how their inquisitiveness makes classroom conversations more engaging. I love how diverse Asperger's can be.

The traits I listed here, and elsewhere in this book, aren't present in every child with Asperger's, and can occur in any combination. These kids are all unique, fascinating, and always make a lasting impression on me. I learn as much from them as, hopefully, they learn from me.

I'm sure you could add many more observations to this list, and I encourage you to do so, often.

Disclaimer

Michael Uram and the publisher make no representations or warranties regarding the accuracy or completeness of the contents of this work. They specifically disclaim all warranties, including without limitation warranties of fitness or any harm done to the reader or their children. If you are concerned about whether you are implementing these ideas properly, there are many providers with extensive training that are available for consultation in an office setting, support group, or even in home. Michael has checked these sources, which are believed to be reliable in their efforts to provide clinically sound information that is complete and generally in accordance with the standards of practice that are accepted at the time of publication. There is always the possibility of human error or changes in behavioral, mental health, or medical sciences, especially in this evolving field, which will affect the usefulness of this book. The publisher and author are not responsible for the results obtained from the use of such information. Readers are encouraged to confirm the information contained in this book with other sources.

The information in this book is not a substitute for mental health counseling or consultation with a health-care professional. Each person's health care is their responsibility, and it is their responsibility to seek out consultation with a mental health or otherwise qualified health-care provider.

This work is sold with the understanding that the publisher and author are not engaging in rendering medical, legal, or other professional advice or services. If professional assistance is required, the services of a competent professional person should be sought. Neither the publisher nor the author shall be liable for damages arising herefrom. All individuals, organizations, and websites that are referred to in this work as a citation and/or potential source of further information does not mean that the author or the publisher endorses the information that the individual, organization, or website may provide or recommendations that they make.

Resources

These books greatly influenced my thoughts on Asperger's and parenting. These authors are experts in the field and each has a slightly unique beneficial approach to understanding this condition.

BOOKS FOR PARENTS

Ablon, J. Stuart. *Changeable: How Collaborative Problem Solving Changes Lives at Home, at School, and at Work*. New York: TarcherPerigee, 2018.

Aspy, Ruth, and Grossman, Barry G. *The Ziggurat Model 2.0: A Framework for Designing Comprehensive Interventions for High-Functioning Individuals with Autism Spectrum Disorders*. Shawnee Mission, KS: AAPC, 2011.

Barkley, Russell A. *Defiant Children: A Clinician's Manual for Assessment and Parent Training*. 3rd ed. New York and London: The Guilford Press, 2013.

Barkley, Russell A., and Christine M. Benton. *Your Defiant Child: 8 Steps to Better Behavior*. New York and London: The Guilford Press, 2013.

Greene, Ross W. *The Explosive Child: A New Approach for Understanding and Parenting Easily Frustrated, Chronically Inflexible Children*. New York: HarperCollins, 2014.

Greene, Ross W. Raising *Human Beings: Creating a Collaborative Partnership with Your Child*. New York: Scribner, 2017.

Jackson, L. *Freaks, Geeks and Asperger's Syndrome: A User Guide to Adolescence*. London: Jessica Kingsley Publishers, 2002.

Johnson, Susan. *Hold Me Tight: Seven Conversations for a Lifetime of Love*. New York: Little, Brown and Company and Hachette Book Group, 2008.

Miller, Kelli. *Thriving with ADHD Workbook for Kids: 60 Fun Activities to Help Children Self-Regulate, Focus, and Succeed*. Emeryville, CA: Althea Press, 2018.

Morris, Suzanne D. *Inside the Mind: Understanding and Communicating with Those Who Have Autism, Asperger's, Social Communication Disorder, and ADD*. Bothell, WA: Book Network, 2016.

Myles, Brenda Smith. *High-functioning Autism and Difficult Moments: Practical Solutions for Reducing Meltdowns*. Shawnee Mission, KS: AAPC, 2016.

Myles, Brenda Smith, Melissa L. Trautman, and Ronda L. Schelvan. *The Hidden Curriculum: Practical Solutions for Understanding Unstated Rules in Social Situations*. Shawnee Mission, KS: AAPC, 2004.

Nelsen, Jane. *Positive Discipline: The Classic Guide to Helping Children Develop Self-discipline, Responsibility, Cooperation, and Problem-Solving Skills*. New York: Ballantine, 2006.

Phifer, Lisa Weed, Amanda K. Crowder, Tracy Elsenraat, and Robert Hull. *CBT Toolbox for Children and Adolescents: Over 200 Worksheets & Exercises for Trauma, ADHD, Autism, Anxiety, Depression & Conduct Disorders*. Eau Claire, WI: PESI Publishing & Media, 2017.

Robison, John Elder. *Look Me in the Eye: My Life with Asperger's*. New York: Three Rivers Press, 2008.

Silberman, Steve. *Neurotribes: The Legacy of Autism and the Future of Neurodiversity*. New York: Avery, 2015.

Szalavitz, Maia, and Bruce D. Perry. *Born for Love: Why Empathy Is Essential—and Endangered*. New York: William Morrow, 2011.

Wagner, Lorenz. *The Boy Who Felt Too Much: How a Renowned Neuroscientist and His Son Changed Our View of Autism Forever*. New York: Arcade, 2019.

References

Ablon, J. Stuart. *Changeable: How Collaborative Problem Solving Changes Lives at Home, at School, and at Work*. New York: TarcherPerigee, 2018.

Alfageh, Basma, Kenneth K. C. Man, Frank Besag, Tariq M. Alhawassi, Ian C. K. Wong, and Ruth Brauer, R. "Psychotropic Medication Prescribing for Neuropsychiatric Comorbidities in Individuals Diagnosed with Autism Spectrum Disorder (ASD) in the UK." *Journal of Autism and Developmental Disorders* 50, no. 9836 (2020): 1–9. doi: 10.1007/s10803-019-04291-8.

American Psychiatric Association. *Diagnostic and Statistical Manual of Mental Disorders: DSM-IV*. Washington, D.C.: American Psychiatric Association, 1994.

——. *Diagnostic and Statistical Manual of Mental Disorders: DSM-IV-TR*. Washington, DC: American Psychiatric Association, 2000.

——. *Diagnostic and Statistical Manual of Mental Disorders: DSM-5*. 5th ed. Washington, DC: American Psychiatric Association, 2013.

Barkley, Russell A. *12 Principles for Raising a Child with ADHD*. New York and London: The Guilford Press, 2021.

Barkley, Russell A., and Christine M. Benton. *Your Defiant Child: 8 Steps to Better Behavior*. New York and London: The Guilford Press, 2013.

Baron-Cohen, Simon. The Truth about Hans Asperger's Nazi Collusion. *Nature Magazine, Scientific American* (May 2018). ScientificAmerican.com /article/the-truth-about-hans-aspergers-nazi-collusion.

Beck, Judith S. *Cognitive Behavior Therapy: Basics and Beyond*. 3rd ed. New York and London: The Guilford Press, 2021.

Burns, David D. *Feeling Great: The Revolutionary New Treatment for Depression and Anxiety*. Eau Claire, WI: PESI Publishing & Media, 2020.

Campbell, Jonathan M. "Diagnostic Assessment of Asperger's Disorder: A Review of Five Third-Party Rating Scales." *Journal of Autism and Developmental Disorders* 35, no. 1 (Feb. 2005): 25–35. doi: 10.1007 /s10803-004-1028-4.

Cooper, John, Timothy Heron, and William Heward, W. *Applied Behavior Analysis*. 3rd ed. Hoboken, NJ: Pearson Education, 2019.

Czech, Herwig "Response to 'Non-complicit: Revisiting Hans Asperger's Career in Nazi-era Vienna.'" *Journal of Autism and Developmental Disorders* 49, no. 9 (June 2019): 3883–87. doi: 10.1007/s10803-019-04106-w.

Delahooke, M. *Beyond Behaviors: Using Brain Science and Compassion to Understand and Solve Children's Behavioral Challenges*. Eau Claire, WI: PESI Publishing & Media, 2019.

Falk, Dean. "Non-Complicit: Revisiting Hans Asperger's Career in Nazi-era Vienna." *Journal of Autism and Developmental Disorders* 50 (2020): 2573–84. doi: 10.1007/s10803-019-03981-7.

Freedman, Brian, Luther G. Kalb, Benjamin Zablotsky, Elizabeth A. Stuart. "Relationship Status among Parents of Children with Autism Spectrum Disorders: A Population-Based Study." *Journal of Autism and Developmental Disorders* 42, no. 4 (2011): 539–48. doi: 10.1007/s10803-011-1269-y.

Friedberg, Robert, and Jessica M. McClure. *Clinical Practice of Cognitive Therapy with Children and Adolescents: The Nuts and Bolts*. 2nd ed. New York and London: The Guilford Press, 2018.

Gabriele, Stefano, Roberto Sacco, and Antonio Persico. "Blood Serotonin Levels in Autism Spectrum Disorder: A Systematic Review and Meta-Analysis." *European Neuropsychopharmacology* 24, no. 6 (June 2014): 919–29. doi: 10.1016/j.euroneuro.2014.02.004.

Gardner, Howard. *5 Minds for the Future*. Harvard Busines School Publishing, 2006.

Grandin, Temple. *Temple Talks . . . about Autism and Sensory Issues: The World's Leading Expert on Autism Shares Her Advice and Experiences*. Arlington, TX: Sensory World, 2015.

Greene, Ross W. *Lost at School: Why Our Kids with Behavioral Challenges Are Falling through the Cracks and How We Can Help Them*. New York: Scribner, 2014.

——. *The Explosive Child: A New Approach for Understanding and Parenting Easily Frustrated, Chronically Inflexible Children*. New York: HarperCollins, 2014.

Kilroy, Emilly, Lisa Aziz-Zadeh, and Sharon Cermak. "Ayres Theories of Autism and Sensory Integration Revisited: What Contemporary Neuro-science Has to Say." *Brain Sciences* 9, no. 3 (Mar. 2019): 68. doi: 10.3390/brainsci9030068.

McNeil, Cheryl Bodiford, and Toni L. Hembree-Kigin, T. L. *Parent-Child Interaction Therapy*. 2nd ed. New York: Springer Nature, 2010.

Markram, Kamila, and Henry Markram. "The Intense World Theory—A Unifying Theory of the Neurobiology of Autism." *Frontiers in Human Neuroscience* 4 (Dec. 2010). doi: 10.3389/fnhum.2010.00224.

Mesibov, Gary B., Victoria Shea, and Eric Schopler. *The TEACCH Approach to Autism Spectrum Disorders*. New York: Springer, 2004.

Morris, Suzanne D. *Inside the Mind: Understanding and Communicating with Those Who Have Autism, Asperger's, Social Communication Disorder, and ADD*. Bothell, WA: Book Publishers Network, 2016.

Olinkiewicz, Alex. "In My Mind (A Video about Asperger's/Autism)." March 29, 2007. YouTube video, 4:15. youtu.be/rbgUjmeC-4o.

Piwowarczyk, Anna, Andrea Horvath, Jan Łukasik, Ewa Pisula, and Hania Szajewska. "Gluten- and Casein-free Diet and Autism Spectrum Disorders in Children: A Systematic Review." *European Journal of Nutrition* 57, no. 5 (June 2017): 433–40. doi: 10.1007/s00394-017-1483-2.

Rogers, Sally J., and Geraldine Dawson. *Early Start Denver Model for Young Children with Autism: Promoting Language, Learning, and Engagement*. New York and London: The Guilford Press, 2010.

Sanchack, Kristian, and Craig A. Thomas. "Autism Spectrum Disorder: Primary Care Principles." *American Family Physician* 94, no. 12 (2016): 972–79.

Silberman, Steve. *NeuroTribes: The Legacy of Autism and the Future of Neurodiversity*. New York: Avery, 2016.

Szalavitz, Maia, and Bruce D. Perry. *Born for Love: Why Empathy Is Essential—and Endangered*. New York: William Morrow, 2011.

Wright, Peter, W. D., Pamela Darr Wright, and Sandra Webb O'Connor. *Wrightslaw: All about IEPs*. Hartfield, VA: Harbor House Law Press, 2015.

Xie, Sherlly, Hakan Karlsson, Christina Dalman, Linnea Widman, Dheeraj Rai, Renee M. Gardner, Cecilia Magnusson, C., Diana E. Schendel, Craig J. Newschaffer, and Brian K. Lee. "Family History of Mental and Neurological Disorders and Risk of Autism." *JAMA Network Open* 2, no. 3 (Mar. 2019): e190154. doi: 10.1001/jamanetworkopen.2019.0154.

WEBSITES

AANE: Asperger / Autism Network. AANE.org.

Autism Key. "Meditation and Mindfulness for Autism." AutismKey.com/meditation-and-mindfulness-for-autism.

Autism Speaks. AutismSpeaks.org.

Center for Parent Information & Resources. ParentCenterHub.org.

Great! Schools.org. GreatSchools.org.

The Incredible Years. IncredibleYears.com.

Dr. Alan E. Kazdin, The Kazdin Method of Parenting. AlanKazdin.com.

TACA: The Autism Community in Action. TACANow.org.

Taylor Bug Kisses Foundation. TaylorBugKisses.com.

Think:Kids. ThinkKids.org.

Michael Uram, MA, LMFT, LPCC. MichaelUram.com.

The Zones of Regulation. ZonesOfRegulation.com.

Index

Acknowledgments

I would like to thank every client I've worked with who has taught me something new about Asperger's. It has been an honor to be allowed into your life with my purpose of helping you be more you. I would like to thank Sara Gardner, Debra Ann Afarian, Debora Smith and family, Rodney Ziebol, Coco Stanbech, Nancy Schramm, Nellie Valentine, Danielle Wiltchik, Catherine Butler, Juhi Sharma, Doris and Rick Bowman, Erik Kola, Beth Holliman, and all the other professionals and parent group facilitators I have learned from over the years. I would like to thank my wife and children, Angelique, Grayson, and Cameron, for allowing me to balance work and home life. I love our adventures together all over the world, whether it is going to Evian, Jerusalem, London, Pompei, Rome, Disneyland, or San Diego.

About the Author

Michael Uram, MA, LMFT, LPCC, is the founder of Uram Family Therapy, which offers individual, couples, and family therapy in Orange County, California. He has established a unique private practice that emphasizes helping clients be more themselves and respecting their desires and boundaries while helping them grow one percent each day. He holds a master's degree in clinical psychology from Pepperdine University in Malibu, California. He supervises a staff that uses the principles on which he founded his practice. Rajiv Joshi, Cristina Deneve, and, previously, Debra Sussman have helped him grow his understanding of how to adapt his theories and practice to a broad audience. He specializes in treating ADHD, Asperger's, OCD, anxiety, and depression through the use of cognitive behavioral therapy, collaborative problem-solving, and whichever theory has the most evidence to help his clients. He has experience using trauma-informed, evidence-based interventions.

Printed in the USA
CPSIA information can be obtained
at www.ICGtesting.com
LVHW060055111023
760753LV00007B/179